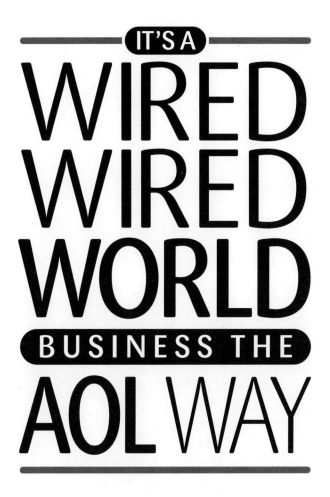

DAVID STAUFFER

IT'S A
WIRED WIRED WORLD
BUSINESS THE
AOL WAY

CAPSTONE

First published 2000 by
Capstone Publishing, Inc.
40 Commerce Park
Milford
CT 06460
USA
Contact: info@capstonepub.com

Capstone Publishing Limited
Oxford Centre for Innovation
Mill Street
Oxford OX2 0JX
United Kingdom
http://www.capstone.co.uk

CIP catalogue records for this book are available from the British Library and the US Library of Congress.
Library of Congress Card Number: 00-104761

ISBN 1-84112-090-1

Typeset in 11/15 pt New Baskerville by
Sparks Computer Solutions Ltd, Oxford, UK
http://www.sparks.co.uk
Printed and bound in the USA by
Sheridan Books, Ann Arbor, Michigan

This book is printed on acid-free paper

Substantial discounts on bulk quantities of Capstone books are available to corporations, professional associations and other organizations. If you are in the USA or Canada, phone the LPC Group, Special Sales Department for details on (1-800-626-4330) or fax (1-800-334-3892). Everywhere else, phone Capstone Publishing on (+44-1865-811113) or fax (+44-1865-240941).

CONTENTS

PREFACE

The greatest frustration in writing a book about America Online and its CEO, Steve Case, is being unable to conclude by reporting the most-deserved "I told you so!" in world history.

Harry Truman gloried in his famous version of "I told you so" the day after defeating Thomas Dewey for the US presidency in 1948, when no one but Truman and (perhaps) his immediate family believed he had even the sliver of a chance to win. The US Olympic hockey team reveled in an "I-told-you-so" group hug and collapse at center ice when they defeated an "unbeatable" Soviet team in 1980.

But no such display – not even the issuance of an under-the-breath "gotcha" – emanates from Steve Case or the very few others who have believed in AOL since the company's earliest days. Yet, oh-how-deserved it would be. "For years, the technology cognoscenti wrote off America Online as dead," executive recruiters Thomas J. Neff and James M. Citrin write – much as hundreds of other commentators have in the past three years or so – in their 1999 book *Lessons From the Top: The Search for America's Best Business Leaders*. "Nobody talks about AOL's imminent demise anymore."[1]

No, today the talk is not of whether AOL can long survive in this world, but of whether the world can long survive the suffocating media domination that a soon-to-be-merged AOL and Time Warner will inflict on all peoples of Earth. Steve Case – having endured for a decade the derision of his supposedly rickety, gasping, out-of-touch enterprise, only to see it rise from its sickbed and be termed an unstoppable "War-of-the-Worlds" invader – is well justified if he wonders just what levels of corporate size and strength might gain a generally approving consensus from those

AOL'S SUBSCRIBER AND SHARE PRICE ROCKET-RIDE [2]

There are too few superlatives to describe AOL's growth. Press accounts seem to use the word "unprecedented" an unprecedented number of times. The charts here report but two ways – albeit important ones – of measuring the company's ascent from square one (on 19 March 1992, the day of its initial public offering) to stratosphere.

Subscriber growth

Year-end	Subscribers	Year's % increase	% Increase since IPO
(19-Mar-92)	150,000	NA	NA
1992	219,000	46	46
1993	531,000	142	254
1994	1,578,000	197	952
1995	4,671,000	167	3,014
1996	7,852,000	196	5,135
1997	10,722,000	37	7,048
1998	15,086,000	41	9,957
1999	20,500,000	36	13,567

Share price growth

Year-end	Share price	Year's % increase	% Increase over IPO
(19-Mar-92)	0.11	NA	NA
1992	0.22	100	100
1993	0.47	114	327
1994	0.88	87	700
1995	2.35	167	2,036
1996	2.07	-12	1,782
1997	5.60	171	4,991
1998	40.00	614	36,263
1999	75.88	90	68,882

who have found AOL too weak one minute and too strong the next.

But Case seems not to be in his line of work for the sake of winning high regard from anyone but his customers. This is why he hasn't – and won't – blurt, "I told you so." Which is but one reason why, in turn, his brand of business leadership is unusual, admirable, and well worth emulating. But writing about it is frustrating.

"For years, the technology cognoscenti wrote off America Online as dead … Nobody talks about AOL's imminent demise anymore."
– *Lessons from the Top*

AUTHOR'S NOTE

While this book was being prepared, AOL declined my request

for interviews of Steve Case and other top honchos – saying that officers of the company were preoccupied with the Time Warner merger. My research was greatly aided, however, by AOL's New York City media relations office, which kindly responded to my numerous inquiries regarding the company's history and financial performance. I appreciate their efforts.

NOTES

1.   Thomas J. Neff and James M. Citrin, *Lessons from the Top: The Search for America's Best Business Leaders*, Currency-Doubleday, New York, 1999.

2.   AOL corporate Website (http://www.corp.aol.com).

Introduction

AOL: A MODEL FOR 21ST CENTURY SURVIVAL AND SUCCESS

D o you look forward to managing a business in the 21st century? Your answer may be "yes" – if you happen to like, say, bungee jumping, kick boxing, and other so-called extreme sports.

It's survival of the fittest in global commerce these days, to an extent so intensely Darwinian that Darwin himself – who witnessed first-hand the life-or-death struggles of living things the world over – might avert his eyes. Today's corporate carnage can just as easily bring down the world's largest and longest-lived businesses as its fledgling enterprises.

How bad can it be for business leaders in our new millennium? According to business school professors David Yoffie and Michael Cusumano, writing in the *Harvard Business Review*:

> "... the Internet forces managers and employees to change their ideas, experiment, invent, and plan constantly, while they try to build complex new products and technologies. The Internet also requires companies to face the reality that competitive advantage can appear and disappear overnight ... Without speed and flexibility, very few companies can compete successfully on Internet time ...

> "[However,] several core elements of competitive advantage ... remain critical to the overall equation for creating a successful company, even in the most turbulent of environments."[1]

AOL IN BRIEF[2]

- *Founded:* 1985
- *Primary business:* interactive services, Web brands, Internet technologies, and e-commerce services.
- *Subscribers:* more than 22 million (about 10 times as many as Microsoft's MSN).
- *Scope:* offers services in 15 countries and seven languages.
- *Headquarters:* near Washington Dulles Airport in the Northern Virginia suburbs of Washington, DC
- *Employees:* 12,100
- *Annual revenues (fiscal 1999):* $4.8 billion (more than the next 20 Internet companies combined)
- *Profit (fiscal 1999):* $762 million
- *IPO:* March 19, 1992
- *Market value:* about $165 billion on 1/1/2000, bigger than any other media concern in the world.
- *Stock symbol:* AOL (New York Stock Exchange)
- *Stock appreciation:* almost 69,000% from IPO to 1/1/2000, tops among all US publicly traded stocks for the 1990s.
- *Brands:* Internet service providers America Online and CompuServe; specialized services ICQ, AOL Instant Messenger, and Digital City, Inc.; portals Netscape Netcenter and AOL.com; browsers Netscape Navigator and Communicator; movie listing and ticketing service AOL MovieFone; Internet music services Spinner Networks and NullSoft, Inc.
- *Named by:* Steve Case, who won the employee naming contest he organized.
- *Website:* AOL.com

But how are you, the business executive, to know what's new and what's unchanged in the Internet economy? You can probably do no better than look to the example of AOL for guidance.

A COMPANY THAT MEETS TODAY'S CHALLENGES

To say America Online has not just survived, but thrived, in the brave new world of brutal corporate competition is to make an understatement of staggering proportions. The company led by Steve Case – himself an entrepreneurial competitor since a boyhood filled with newspaper delivery, lemonade stands, and magazine sales – has done everything wrong in terms of conventional business wisdom, and everything right in terms of what companies must do to succeed in an Internet-enabled global economy.

> During prime time, the number of people logged on to AOL is more than are watching top-drawing cable networks such as MTV and CNN.

Consider only a few of the mind-blowing achievements of this company that's still under the age at which most states will issue a driver's license:[3]

- AOL's market valuation is greater than that of the entire publicly-traded US newspaper industry.

- AOL has more subscribers than *Time*, *Newsweek*, and *US News & World Report* combined.

- Almost 40% of the time that all Americans spend on the

AOL'S CORPORATE TIME LINE[4]

1985

- Founded as Quantum Computer Services, offering an online service called Q-Link for owners of Commodore computers.

1986

- Q-Link subscribers number 100,000, owing to Case's persistence in marketing, but Commodore is already a sinking ship.

1987–8

- Quantum allies with Apple. The newly introduced Macintosh computer offers Q-Link as its only online service.

1989

- Q-Link service is renamed America Online, a Mac-only service that offers games, e-mail, chat rooms, and some news articles.
- Apple and Quantum split in an acrimonious divorce.

1991

- The corporate name Quantum Computer is dropped in favor of America Online, the name by which the public knows it.
- Quantum board of directors replaces Case with James Kimsey as CEO, believing the latter, older executive would more favorably impress investors than the 32-year-old Case.

1992

- Initial public offering in March raises $66 million.
- Steve Case succeeds Jim Kimsey as CEO.
- AOL's 200,000 subscribers put it a distant third in popularity behind CompuServe and Prodigy.
- Employees number 250.

1993

- Version of AOL for Microsoft's Windows operating system is introduced.

- Marc Andreessen co-founds Netscape.
- Stock wins first high-profile buy rating from Morgan Stanley analyst Mary Meeker.

1994

- Buys Redgate Communications, whose founder, Theodore J. Leonsis, joins and still serves in AOL top management.
- Gains 1 millionth subscriber.

1995

- Teams up with German media firm Bertelsmann to offer online services in Europe.
- The empire strikes back: Windows 95 is launched with bundled software for MSN and Explorer Web browser.

1996

- Reaches 5 million subscribers.
- Case makes *Business Week*'s cover; inside, AOL is termed the "most potent force in cyberspace."
- Network goes off line for 19 hours. Company writes off $385 million in highly controversial deferred subscriber acquisition costs. Stock falls 52% during last half of the year.
- Stock trading moves to New York Stock Exchange.
- Scuttles hourly use charge in favor of unlimited-use pricing plan at $19.95 a month.
- Hires MTV co-founder Robert W. Pittman to run online service.

1997

- Surpasses 10 million subscribers.

1998

- Buys CompuServe, a competing pioneering online service that once had six times as many subscribers as AOL.
- Subscribers for the first time ever cumulatively log 10 million hours of use in a single day, as 800,000 of them download the report on President Clinton and Whitewater issued by special prosecutor Kenneth Starr.

- Agrees to buy Netscape.
- Added to the S&P 500 Index.

1999

- Buys Netscape Communications Corp., whose Navigator browser popularized the World Wide Web.
- Buys MovieFone Inc., the nation's largest movie listing guide and ticketing service.
- Invests $1.5 billion in DirecTV creator Hughes Electronics to develop and market high-speed services via satellite.
- Surpasses 20 million subscribers. ICQ messaging service surpasses 50 million registered users.

2000

- *January:* announces planned merger with Time Warner Inc.

Web is spent within the friendly confines of AOL content and services.

- On weeknights during prime time, the number of people logged on to AOL peaks at about 1 million, more than are watching top-drawing cable networks such as MTV and CNN.

- Users spend an average of more than an hour a day logged on to AOL, compared with only a quarter-hour as recently as 1996.

And now, pending combination with Time Warner, AOL is poised to become a media titan of unprecedented size and scope.

A COMPANY THAT LEAVES EXPERTS SPUTTERING

A thorough review of expert opinion on AOL throughout the 1990s reveals consensus on one matter above all others: AOL is at the brink of its final decline and fall. Seers confidently state, again and again, that the company's plunge into oblivion will commence next month. Okay, maybe next year, or perhaps in three years at most.

Well, experts thus far have been just as right about AOL as they were about our need for candles and canned goods at the stroke of midnight, Y2K. Here's a sampling of opinion:

> "America Online will probably never catch up in size with Prodigy or CompuServe."
> – *Business Week*, 1992

- "With its niche strategy, America Online will probably never catch up in size with Prodigy or CompuServe." – *Business Week*, September 14 1992[5]

- "By the end of the decade, the report [from the research firm Jupiter Communications] said, AOL and Prodigy 'will experience both declining market share and slower annual growth rates than their newer competitors.' Jupiter expects that major media or telecommunications companies, such as … Time Warner Inc. … will seize the market …" – *The Washington Post*, November 8 1993[6]

- "Don't look now, but Prodigy, AOL, and CompuServe are all suddenly obsolete – and Mosaic is well on its way to becoming the world's standard interface." – *Wired* magazine, October 1994[7]

- "Even Steve Case's best scrambling can't prop AOL's stock forever. Someday, he's going to have to score by showing real profits or pull off a financial Hail Mary miracle play by selling AOL. Know a good, hungry phone company?" – Columnist Allan Sloan in *Newsweek*, May 27 1996[8]

- "[AOL's] attitude toward the Web is a little grouchy. They have a hard time getting past their own resentment that this disorganized cousin is taking over in the public's mind. But it is a bias against inescapable realities." – Forrester Research director Emily Green, quoted in *Forbes* magazine, October 7 1996[9]

- "[I]t's true that AOL will not die a quick and sudden death. But it may well fade out, lumbering in the background as the service of choice for the least savvy users … It might, in other words, persist. But just going on is not nearly as sexy, or as profitable, as dominating." – Stefanie Syman, executive editor of the online magazine *FEED*, writing in *The Wall Street Journal*, September 15 1997[10]

These experts and countless more were dead wrong about AOL. What does Steve Case know – or believe – that they missed? He knows how to compete and win in the Internet age. He knows, in other words, the keys to success that are revealed in the following pages.

HOW AOL – AND CASE – MADE IT HAPPEN

The stories of how AOL and Steve Case confounded the experts and succeeded when no one thought they should have been recounted and analyzed in mountains of articles, books, and analysts' reports. From these many sources and viewpoints, ten secrets of AOL's success emerge.

1. Go into everybody's business

Among a select few in entrepreneurial history, Henry Ford did it with the Model T, Ted Turner with CNN, and Steve Case with AOL. They had the prescience – and/or great luck – to know that tens of millions of people would want a certain product long before those people had any notion what that product was. Case – while criss-crossing the US sampling new pizza toppings for Pizza Hut – plugged his clunky Kaypro computer into phone jacks, went online at a speed matching the flow rate of a tar pit, and knew in his bones that people everywhere would one day clamor for access to cyberspace.

2. Give your business a human face

By personality, Steve Case is about the least likely of corporate CEOs to serve as the human face of a business far removed from a humanizing touch, feel, or emotion. He's variously described as introverted, distant, even aloof. But he was able from his first days online to understand that the experience for most people wouldn't be about Macs, modems, and megabytes. He knew instead that the vast majority of us would be persuaded to link with cyberspace on the promise of establishing, keeping, and deepening our connections with other people. Case recognized, almost alone, that high-tech is little more than pavement on the road to high touch.

3. Never be dissuaded from pursuing your dream

In 1980, recent college graduate Steve Case stated his always-and-ever-succinct vision of a wired world in job-hunting cover letters: Innovations in telecommunications, he wrote, will result in our television sets becoming an information line, newspaper, school, computer, referendum machine, and catalog. One such letter went to HBO, recently acquired by Time Inc. and then headed by Gerald Levin – with whom Case would deal on very different terms two decades later. Had Levin held on to that letter, it could have as accurately expressed Case's vision in 2000 as it had years earlier. Case's dream of a wired world – little altered as AOL's mission statement – is the driving force by which AOL came to be known as "the cockroach of cyberspace," scurrying about, little noticed by the corporate Goliaths, surviving and growing as the giants faded or fell.

4. KISS! Keep it simple, stupid!

How familiar – and true – the phrase is; how little practiced by most companies – particularly those in high-tech dazzled by the complex wizardry they can demonstrate in their product and service offerings. AOL understands, better than any other prominent new-media company, that the *ability* to provide gee-whiz technological gimmicks says absolutely nothing about whether consumers *want* them. AOL is content to take a pass on the hot new enhancements that are a geek's greatest joy, but would frustrate Aunt Hattie. This is the dopey, lumbering Internet company for everyone outside Silicon Valley.

5. Ignore "irrelevant" experts - customers rule!

If Internet analysts and Silicon sages are right, then AOL has done everything wrong in its eight-year surge from insignificance to unprecedented success. How could it have happened? There's no mystery – or even brilliance, for that matter – in Steve Case's opinion: AOL simply listened to customers. That's not particularly difficult, or expensive. Yet it seems many companies would rather spend a fortune telling the world they're customer-focused than implement the sort of ongoing effort by which AOL makes customer focus happen.

6. Don't shy from a fight ...

In May 1993, Steve Case – tenuous CEO of tenuous, unprofitable, market-lagging AOL – sat across from Microsoft's Bill Gates for the first time ever and heard these words: "I can buy 20 percent of you or I can buy all of you. Or I can go into this business myself and bury you." Case could have persuaded his board to sell and retired rich. But where would that have left his dream of taking the world into its wired future? So he, in effect, invited Gates to bury him – and led AOL to the most clear-cut victory over Microsoft yet realized by any company still around to tell its tale. It was only the first time AOL and Case would demonstrate a resolve and combativeness that have vanquished all challengers.

7. ... Or hesitate to sleep with the enemy

The world in which you could always depend on Pepsi hating Coke, Avis battling Hertz, and Wile E. Coyote scheming to get the Road Runner is gone. With today's fickle consumers, lightning-fast product cycles, and incessant change, alliances and acquisitions must always be front-burner considerations for any nimble enterprise. And AOL in this regard is among the nimblest. The company has stunned observers, competitors, and others in announcing alliances with the likes of Microsoft and AT&T and acquisitions of the likes of CompuServe and Netscape. As usual, however, there's plenty of method and no madness in AOL's partnering and purchasing; all such moves are consistent with the firm's mission.

8. Leverage successes, build your brands

AOL has so masterfully practiced synergy in building its business that a whole new word, defined as "super-synergy" seems to be needed. Its brilliant moves range from blatant – covering the earth with millions of free-trial computer disks – to subtle – using chat rooms to encourage subscribers to self-segregate according to special interests and be exposed to highly targeted advertising. Benefiting from the consumer insights of president and COO Bob Pittman, AOL in only a few years has become a brand-building firm of Disney-like stature.

9. Admit mistakes and grow forward

AOL has made bonehead moves of a consequence and frequency that have felled more than a few other firms. And yet it has surged ahead in its growth and popularity – seeming to be rewarded for mistakes rather than paying for them. What gives? The company offers textbook lessons in how to steer the perfect middle course between shrugging at the harm its goofs have caused and prostrating itself in begging forgiveness. Mistakes go hand-in-hand with bold growth; they provide clear feedback on what customers and the public will and won't tolerate; and – handled right – they can even help to humanize a company.

10. Get to the future today

There was a time when companies had time to perceive, measure, and then react to changes in customer preferences. Only a few years ago, the pace picked up: companies had to find ways to change in lockstep with customers – delay could mean death. Today, the required speed of change for companies can exceed that of customers: You've got to anticipate where customer demand is heading and be there *before* they arrive. AOL is perhaps the world's outstanding example of a company that's been ready with what customers want before the customers knew they wanted it. When AOL badly trailed CompuServe and Prodigy in market share, Steve Case was certain people wanted simplicity and connections with other people in their online experience. When it seemed the whole world saw the Web as the instrument of AOL's death, Case was sure most users would willingly pay for a guide to that vast new world. Time and again, Case and AOL have gotten to the future ahead of everyone.

NOTES

1. David Yoffie and Michael Cusumano, "Judo Strategy: The Competitive Dynamics of Internet Time," *Harvard Business Review*, January/February 1999.

2. Compiled from numerous reports and AOL corporate Website (http://www.corp.aol.com).

3. Compiled from numerous reports.

4. Compiled from numerous reports.

5. Mark Lewyn, "For America Online, Nothing Is as Nice as a Niche," *Business Week*, September 14, 1992.

6. Daniel Southerland, "America Online's Rapid Rise," *The Washington Post*, November 8, 1993.

7. Gary Wolfe, "The (Second Phase of the) Revolution Has Begun," *Wired*, October 1994.

8. Allan Sloan, "Spooking the Street," *Newsweek*, May 27, 1996.

9. Gene Koprowski, "AOL CEO Steve Case," *Forbes ASAP*, October 7, 1996.

10. Stefanie Syman, "Is America Online a Leviathan or a Dinosaur?" *The Wall Street Journal*, September 15, 1997.

One

GO INTO EVERYBODY'S BUSINESS

IN THIS CHAPTER

The Internet was an unnamed infant when Steve Case abandoned a promising marketing career in an established industry to cast his lot with nothing more than the potential for making a living from cyberspace. But the 24-year-old Case wasn't chasing rainbows. Instead, as *The Washington Times* would later report, he "sensed the vast potential for the Internet as a means for people to gather information and communicate."[1]

He would need the courage of his convictions time and again in the years that followed, as early failures, missteps, and dead ends would probably have defeated anyone less certain of his vision. This chapter tells how a determined entrepreneur pictured the rise of a new industry and rode out all setbacks until it happened.

Persistence is an admirable trait that often occupies a narrow space between flightiness and obsession. The entrepreneur who flits from one consumer fad to another is unlikely to achieve lasting success in any of them, while the one who doggedly insists that manual typewriters are sure to make a comeback might be considered a candidate for institutionalization.

If Steve Case had been either less certain that the world would eventually clamor to be online or very certain that everyone would want to enter the new millennium with hula hoops or pet rocks, we'd never have heard of him (at least in any favorable way) or, in all likelihood, America Online.

But Case had the right vision for the right reasons and held onto it long enough for the rest of humanity to eventually see things his way. Here's what the then-21-year-old, job-seeking, new college grad wrote in his 1980 cover letters to CEOs of media-related firms for whom he hoped to work:

> "I firmly believe that technological advances in communications are on the verge of significantly altering our way of life ... Innovations in telecommunications (especially two-way cable systems) will result in our television sets (big screen, of course!) becoming an information line, newspaper, school, computer, referendum machine, and catalog."[2]

How remarkable is this bold claim? Consider that the fax was still a primitive spinning drum, there were no cable TV networks, and the PC was still a few years from its first sale! Further, Case's view of the future failed to win employment from, among others, HBO. His letter to that firm, newly owned by Time Inc., was addressed to none other than Gerald Levin, who 20 years later would accept terms under which Case would become chairman and he CEO of AOL Time Warner, in the then-world's largest-ever corporate merger.

One can only wonder whether, at any time in the Case–Levin discussions of late 1999 and 2000, the Time Warner chief said, "Gee, Steve, you were right on target twenty years ago."

LOOK FOR POTENTIAL, NOT PROFIT, IN NASCENT INDUSTRIES

Steve Case didn't chuck his marketing job in PepsiCo's Pizza Hut unit in 1983 to join a flourishing online industry. Quite to

the contrary, he signed on with an eccentric, unproven entrepreneur (named Bill Von Meister) in a shaky enterprise (called
Control Video Corp.) operating in a virtually nonexistent business (distributing Atari video games to home computers via
telephone lines).[3] The move prompted Case's father to observe
that, "Job hoppers don't wind up anywhere." And, the elder
Case opined, "this new job seems a little crazy."[4]

But Case was convinced he was onto something. People everywhere, he figured, would want two-way interactive electronic
links to information and other people, provided the mecha-
nism allowing those links was simple and affordable. Trouble
was, of course, that neither he nor anyone else could know
what equipment and technologies would provide such links
before they'd been invented. So he signed on with a company
that looked like it might be heading in the right direction and,
not incidentally, would overlook his youth and inexperience
and entrust him with the marketing by which the enterprise
would sink or swim.

Case also understood then – as he does to this day – that it's
not smart to expect or even want significant profitability in a
business that has captured only a fraction of its potential customer universe. As recently as 1996 he noted that barely more
than one in ten US households subscribe to online services.
"The mass market for these services is only beginning to
emerge," he argued. "So we shouldn't slow down and maxi-
mize profits from our existing members."[5]

It's important to note that Case, apparently unlike many other
leaders of Internet start-ups, eschews profit *maximizing*, but not
profits themselves. Further, he implicitly recognizes that, in
today's Internet-speed business world, we've compressed our

STEVE'S STUTTERING START IN ONLINE ENTERPRISE[6]

Although Steve Case was probably among the first people on the planet to realistically envision a wired world, he at first had little idea how or where it would develop. He's experienced the trials and tribulations of getting online with these corporate entities:

- *Control Video*
  Steve Case joined Control Video Corp. after meeting its founder, Bill Von Meister, at a Las Vegas electronics exposition in 1983. Case's job was marketing CVC's online service – distributing Atari video games to computers via telephone lines. Two weeks after Case arrived, the firm's capital dried up. CVC shareholders forced Von Meister out (spared Case by "a narrow margin") and hired West Pointer and Vietnam veteran Jim Kimsey, who was as straight-shooting and rigid as Von Meister was eccentric and impulsive.

- *Quantum Computer Services*
  Restructuring and an infusion of new financing led to CVC's re-birth in 1985 as Quantum Computer Services Inc., which marketed an online bulletin board for owners of Commodore 64 comput-ers. It would have been a tough sell for anyone, as Commodore was past its peak and heading for oblivion. Nonetheless, Case plugged away, gaining 10,000 subscribers for the online service – now called Q-Link – by January 1986.
  Quantum broke its identification with Commodore by allying with Apple Computer in time for Q-Link to be the only online service offered with the Apple Macintosh during that computer model's sensational early years. But the Apple-Quantum relationship gradu-ally deteriorated, coming to an end in 1989.

- *OLA?*

  With Quantum facing the prospect of independence from any computer maker, Kimsey and Case decided that Q-Link needed a facelift. They announced a contest among employees to come up with a new name for the service and, according to Canada's *National Post*, "Case thought of Online America, flipped the words around, and declared himself the contest winner."

- *AOL!*

  The Mac-only online service called America Online began offering games, e-mail, chat rooms, and news articles in 1989. Two years later, with the service well known and the company not, the corporate name Quantum Computer Services was dropped in favor of America Online Inc. Case was CEO, but was mistaken if he thought he'd at last found his proper seat at the online revolution. The board soon replaced him with Kimsey, who they thought better fulfilled Wall Street's image of what a CEO should look like than did the 32-year-old Case. The demotion is said to have had no outwardly noticeable adverse effects on Case. And he waited only 13 months until he was reinstalled as CEO – just in time to represent the company at a meeting with Microsoft, where Bill Gates told Case his company could buy or bury the firm at last known far and wide as AOL.

notions of time to the point that we expect global pervasiveness of industries within mere years of their emergence. "Decades from now, when the story of the last years of the 20th century is told," he told a National Press Club audience in 1998, "historians will point to how fast the interactive medium has become a real essential part of everyday life of millions of people all around the world."[7]

Faster even than Case himself might expect? Perhaps, if this assessment by *The Christian Science Monitor*, following announcement of the planned AOL–Time Warner merger, is on the mark: "The World Wide Web's growing importance in daily life can be seen in some of Monday's headlines before the merger was announced. Front pages included stories of how the Internet is spurring the illegal importation of medicine to the US, how a large number of credit-card numbers were stolen and broadcast on a Web site, and how General Motors and Ford are planning to use cyberspace to reach customers."[8]

> **"...the Internet is not an extension of the past, ... it is a new life form altogether."**
> **– Steve Case**

Nonetheless – and despite his rocket ride since accepting a "crazy" job – Case seems to believe the industry he's molding in no small way still shows more future promise than past performance. "Exactly how the Internet will evolve ... is a fascinating mystery. What is clear already, however, is that the Internet is not an extension of the past, not a hybrid of old and new, it is a new life form altogether."[9]

MAKE EARLY FAILURE A LEARNING – NOT LETHAL – EXPERIENCE ...

Steve Case would likely have been excused by anyone if he'd given up on his foray into the world of online services at any one of numerous points when his future or that of his company appeared at best grim. Case, referring to the earliest such point – the collapse of his first online services employer, Control Video Corporation – said, "I arrived [at CVC] just in time for the death of the video game business."[10]

Enough setbacks and disappointments to fill a 10-gig hard drive would follow. But rather than being defeated, Case was learning ever more from them. He learned, for example – as few other entrepreneurs in his business have apparently learned even to this day – that most people want simplicity and user-friendliness, not gimmickry and high-tech obscurity, in an online service. He also learned that people will willingly pay a fee to a company that will take them by the hand and patiently guide them to the information they want, even when they supposedly could pay nothing and get the same information by figuring out the navigation on their own. And he learned, perhaps most importantly of all, that for all but a relative handful of computer geeks, people are attracted to the new interactive media not by the technologies they employ, but by the prospect of employing those technologies to connect with other people.

And it's clear from daring moves such as the AOL–Time Warner merger that Case shows no sign of letting up on an approach to growing his business that flirts with the potential for failure on a scale more spectacular than he's ever before experienced. He understands that being safe from failure means standing still, something Steve Case would hardly do when only a fraction of the world's people are online – and the relative few who are online still spend an average of 23 hours a day offline.

... AND TREAT TRIUMPHS AS FLEETING

In much the same way that good things can happen if you're not defeated by early failure and setbacks, good things are more likely to keep happening if you regard triumphs as transitory. This is probably more true in business today than at any previous time: A company's success – even on a small scale or of quite modest proportions – is closely watched and quickly imitated by any number of current and would-be competitors.

Considering the competitive attacks on AOL from upstarts such as Yahoo and established giants such as AT&T and Microsoft, it's no wonder Steve Case gives every indication that he understands how fleeting success can be in the absence of constant vigilance. For example, three of his central concerns during the recent years of AOL's rocketing growth have been:

- *Balancing AOL's subscription income with ad revenues.* Rather than basking in the plaudits earned by persuading more than 20 million subscribers to pay AOL to be their gateway to interactivity, Case and AOL president Bob Pittman have worked hard to lessen the company's disproportionate income from monthly fees. In mid-1999, AOL was reported to be taking in $19.44 a month per subscriber in fees but only $4.50 in advertising. The target is to eventually make those revenue sources about equal, which means offering content and capabilities that convince users to spend more time online.[11]

The urgency of this effort has increased over the past year or so with the rise of free Internet services from NetZero, Juno Online Services, and – especially in Europe – other brash newcomers who'd like nothing better than stepping into the giant-killer role once occupied by AOL itself. By January 2000 NetZero had gained three million members in less than 15 months, making it the second-largest Internet service provider in the US (though only one-seventh the size of AOL).[12]

• *Anticipating the rise of interactivity using hardware other than PCs.* Even while he was battling to establish his company as the Internet service provider of choice for PC owners, Case was among the first to weigh business implications of non-PC connectivity. As long ago as November 1993, when AOL's future in a PC-based world was still shaky, the company was reported by *The Washington Post* to be striving "to establish an early lead in new markets, such as small, hand-held personal communications devices."[13]

In this instance, also, the imperative for action has only become more pronounced in recent years, as televisions increasingly promise capabilities once limited to PCs (and vice versa) and devices such as cell phones, pagers, and personal electronic organizers handle e-mail, stock quotes, and other features once accessible only via PCs. At the time AOL and Time Warner announced their engagement, *US News & World Report* reported that Case believes "Americans won't discard their computers or their televisions, but the distinction between them will become very fuzzy."[14]

• *Determining AOL's optimum positioning in relation to the Web.* From 1994 to 1996 – a period during which AOL added more subscribers (5 million) than any other Internet service provider has ever had in total subscribers – Case was, according to *Forbes* magazine, "eyeing the World Wide Web skeptically

WHAT STEVE BELIEVES

A look back from the perspective of year 2000 at the record of Steve Case's statements concerning future direction of the Internet and its related technologies reveals jaw-dropping accuracy time and again. Here's a sampling of the AOL chief's correct prognostications that most experts doubted or laughed at when Case made them:

- "I think companies like AOL are well positioned to be the way most Americans connect to the Internet." – Quoted in *Time* magazine, September 26, 1994[18]
- "The investment debate comes down to two different views of the future. One view is that we're a leader in an exciting new field, and we could become another Wal-Mart, Home Depot, or even a Microsoft. The other is that we're a very fragile franchise about to be battered by competition from Microsoft and the Internet. We'll see." – Quoted in *The New York Times*, August 14, 1995[19]
- "A year from now, people will say online services are a superset of the Internet, rather than a competitor of the Internet." – Quoted in *Forbes* magazine, October 7, 1996[20]
- "It is going to take many years before consumers have high-bandwidth access. We will provide a 'virtual broadband service' to people with slow modems. ... The bandwidth gap – the bandwidth haves and bandwidth have-nots – plays right into the hands of AOL." – Quoted in *Forbes* magazine, October 7, 1996[21]
- "In the mid-90s, Steve Case made what seemed at the time to be an outrageous – even ridiculous – prediction: By 2005, he ventured, his company, America Online, would be as big a force on the Internet as Microsoft was in software. The experts had a good laugh. ... No one is laughing now, with the possible exception of Case himself ... [who] now sits atop an online and offline colossus that has made

him the undisputed king of the Internet – a good five years ahead of
schedule." – *US News & World Report*, January 24, 2000[22]

– and more than a little anxiously."[15] Publicly, he was making statements such as this one in a 1994 issue of *Time*
magazine: "We think most people would rather subscribe to
one service, where they can get everything they need through
one interface."[16] Privately, a true-to-form Case and his team
would almost certainly have been examining every conceivable scenario for the Web's future development and
envisioning AOL strategies that would make the company a
major player.

AOL's continuing preoccupation with extending its success
makes it a "roadrunner" company in the eyes of management
consultants Chip R. Bell and Oren Harari, who say such firms
"are road-runner-like, racing down a continuous breakthrough
road." They don't rest on success, because they can't afford to:

> "In the cartoons, you can bet that the Road Runner never as-
> sumes that one breakthrough will ensure permanent success.
> There's always tomorrow, and Wile E. [Coyote] will be skulking
> around with some new scheme, and there'll be some new con-
> traption to 'Beep Beep' through. Without eternal vigilance, and
> without a perpetual commitment to breakthrough, the Road
> Runner might be caught."
>
> *Beep! Beep! Competing in the Age of the Road Runner*
> Chip R. Bell and Oren Harari

AOL and other roadrunner companies, like the Road Runner
himself, "never stop, which is why their ticket is to prosperity."[17]

RESHAPE EVERYTHING BUT YOUR VISION

If ever a business executive was wedded to his way of doing things, he would have resembled Steve Case and AOL's top team in no way whatsoever. As *Newsweek* magazine was moved to comment in 1996, Case "has built AOL into a colossus despite having to change strategies more often than most chief executives change underwear."[23]

Perhaps that in part explains why so many observers have so often predicted the imminent decline of AOL and been so wrong every time. These experts would understandably forecast future events in the life of AOL based on what the company had done in the past. But AOL repeatedly foils prognostications by seeming to do anything *but* what it's done before. "Every time people ask, 'How is [Case] going to survive?' he makes the right moves," the chairman of an Internet software maker told *Business Week* in 1996.[24]

An article in *The Wall Street Journal* the following year reported what may be a typical instance of Case's changing horses in midstream: "He woke up one day and decided his business wasn't about rationing access to a scarce resource; his business was about attracting as many eyeballs as possible to his billboard-lined shopping mall cum singles bar cum newsstand cum mailbox cum anything else the AOL universe wants it to be … Mr. Case's plan has always been to capture the biggest online audience any way he can."[25]

In that last sentence, it would seem, is the constant that underlies the thousand presto-change-o's in the life of AOL. Case and his lieutenants appear true in all of their actions but to one thing: AOL's mission "to build a global medium as essential to people's lives as the telephone and the television – and even more valuable." [26]

The unwavering dedication prompted an unidentified executive of "a rival company" to tell *The San Francisco Chronicle* that Case is "like a metronome. He stuck to his guns, and now he's one of the most powerful people in the industry."[27]

Case had a vision of an interactive future at least as early as 1980 and has demonstrated unwavering dedication to make it happen ever since. The vision needed only minor retooling to serve as AOL's mission, and to serve as a beacon for Case and his company that's fixed more firmly in their heavens than is the North Star in our night sky. *The New York Times*, noting in a 1998 article that, "Littered along [AOL's] path of experimentation and self-discovery are dozens of discarded postures, philosophies, and wounded partners," reported this retort from Case: "Our strategy has been in place for more than a decade … How we execute the strategy has always been in flux."[28]

> "Our strategy has been in place for more than a decade ... How we execute the strategy has always been in flux."
> – Steve Case

The "flux" has provided plenty of opportunity for sniping and sniggering by the press. An earlier *Times* article called attention to a series of changes at AOL that followed another series of changes only one month before: "Yesterday, with the disclosure of another spate of sweeping announcements, [Case] delivered what might be called the *new* new AOL … a new pricing setup, a new management organization, a new top manager, and a new accounting policy."[29]

But reporters and other commentators may not yet understand – at least to the extent that Case seems to understand – that changing course more often than changing underwear is essential to survival in an Internet-speed economy. As David Yoffie and Michael Cusumano noted in a 1999 article in the *Harvard Business Review*, the Internet "allowed Netscape to burst onto the scene in 1994 and, in only a few months, turned the company into one of the most serious threats Microsoft has ever faced."[30]

Facing the ever-present threat of such sudden challenges, an established company has little choice but to be ready at all times for almost instantaneous course changes. The Internet has "realigned the competitive landscape, forcing worried corporations to respond – sometimes hastily – with new ventures and huge deals," *Newsweek* reported in January 2000. [31]

Similarly, *The Wall Street Journal* reported in 1996 that the Internet "has wrought bedlam as companies scurry to find their right place."[32] Perhaps AOL, thanks to having its vision and mission fixed always in its gaze, can occupy its "right place" more readily than any number of would-be competitors.

GO INTO EVERYBODY'S BUSINESS

If you've ever believed deeply in a product idea or consumer trend that no one else seemed to share, you may understand Steve Case's conviction in the early 1980s that the world was pointing toward an interconnected future. Case staked his career on the certainty of his vision, and proceeded to help make it happen by taking these steps to success:

- *Look for potential, not profit, in nascent industries.* You can't kill the goose that laid the golden egg – especially before she's laid it. In working to turn a dream into reality, you've got to favor actions and decisions that promise long-term rewards and tough it out during the early rough-and-tumble times.

- *Make early failure a learning – not lethal – experience ...* There were dead-ends and disappointments aplenty as Case felt his way toward the right corporate structure and strategies before AOL became the rocket that would boost him to triumph. His story is one of business history's great illustrations of refusing to quit in the face of early defeats. Instead, Case's example shows, you pick yourself up, make adjustments based on lessons learned, and jump into the fray once again.

- *... And treat triumphs as fleeting.* Just as Case refused to be defeated by early setbacks, he similarly resisted any urges to become smug or overconfident in the face of mounting successes. The wise course, his example demonstrates, is to understand that the environment in which a victory is won is constantly changing – and you have to continually change your business to keep winning.

- *Reshape everything but your vision.* Observers have made great sport of the continuing stream of strategy shifts by Case and AOL. But the company and its leader appear to understand that, with the continual change in today's world commerce, the company that isn't always changing course is a sitting duck. The take-home lesson here is to keep your eyes on the prize – the vision of what the future will be – and be ever open to any changes that can help you win it.

NOTES

1. Timothy Burn, "Case Gets Last Laugh: AOL Grew From Humble Beginnings," *The Washington Times*, January 11, 2000.

2. Kara Swisher, "How Steve Case Morphed Into a Media Mogul," *The Wall Street Journal*, January 11, 2000.

3. David Akin, "The Winner's Case: Steve Case Has Overcome Many Setbacks," *The National Post*, November 25, 1998.

4. Kara Swisher, "How Steve Case Morphed Into a Media Mogul," *The Wall Street Journal*, January 11, 2000.

5. Gene Koprowski, "AOL CEO Steve Case," *Forbes ASAP*, October 7, 1996.

6. AOL corporate Website (http://www.corp.aol.com); Joshua Cooper Ramo, "How AOL Lost the Battles but Won the War," *Time*, September 22, 1997; David Akin, "The Winner's Case: Steve Case Has Overcome Many Setbacks," *The National Post*, November 25, 1998.

7. Speech at National Press Club, Federal News Service transcript, October 26, 1998.

8. Alexandra Marks and Ron Scherer, "Merger a Landmark of Cyber Age," *The Christian Science Monitor*, January 11, 2000.

9. Speech at National Press Club, Federal News Service transcript, October 26, 1998.

10. Steve Lohr, "Steve Case at a Crossroad," *The New York Times*, August 14, 1995.

11. Saul Hansell, "Now, AOL Everywhere," *The New York Times*, July 4, 1999.

12. Matt Murray, Nikhil Deogun, and Nick Wingfield, "Can Time Warner Click With AOL?" *The Wall Street Journal*, January 14, 2000.

13. Daniel Southerland, "America Online's Rapid Rise," *The Washington Post*, November 8, 1993.

14. Fred Vogelstein, "The Talented Mr Case," *US News & World Report*, January 24, 2000.

15. Gene Koprowski, "AOL CEO Steve Case," *Forbes ASAP*, October 7, 1996.

16. Philip Elmer-dewitt, "Hooked Up to the Max," *Time*, September 26, 1994.

17. Chip R. Bell and Oren Harari, *Beep! Beep! Competing in the Age of the Road Runner*, Warner, New York, 2000.

18. Philip Elmer-dewitt, "Hooked Up to the Max," *Time*, September 26, 1994.

19. Steve Lohr, "Steve Case at a Crossroad," *The New York Times*, August 14, 1995.

20. Gene Koprowski, "AOL CEO Steve Case," *Forbes ASAP*, October 7, 1996.

21. Gene Koprowski, "AOL CEO Steve Case," *Forbes ASAP*, October 7, 1996.

22. Fred Vogelstein, "The Talented Mr. Case," *US News & World Report*, January24, 2000.

23. Allan Sloan, "Spooking the Street," *Newsweek*, May 27, 1996.

24. Amy Cortese and Amy Barrett, "The Online World of Steve Case," *Business Week*, April 15,1996.

25. Holman W. Jenkins Jr, "Maybe AOL's Bankruptcy Would Be More Ethical," *The Wall Street Journal*, April 22, 1997.

26. Speech at National Press Club, Federal News Service transcript, October 26, 1998.

27. Jon Swartz, "Case Study – A Look at Mr. America Online," *The San Francisco Chronicle*, February 22, 1999.

28. Saul Hansell, "America Online's Triumvirate in Cyberspace," *The New York Times*, February 16, 1998.

29. Laurence Zuckerman, "America Online Announces a Newer Transformation," *The New York Times*, October 30, 1996.

30. David Yoffie and Michael Cusumano, "Judo Strategy: The Competitive Dynamics of Internet Time," *Harvard Business Review*, January/February 1999.

31. Johnnie L. Roberts, "Desperately Seeking a Deal," *Newsweek*, January 24, 2000.

32. Jared Sandberg, "America Online Stars in Soap-opera-like Internet Action," *The Wall Street Journal*, March 18, 1996.

Two

GIVE YOUR BUSINESS A HUMAN FACE

IN THIS CHAPTER

How has Steve Case so successfully appealed to AOL's typical customer: the average-Joe-or-Jane, semi-affluent, suburban resident who loves connecting with other people by spending time online? Perhaps – in spite of fame and riches – by so successfully staying true to his genuine self: the average-Joe, semi-affluent, suburban resident who loves connecting with other people by spending time online. And Case has successfully inculcated all of AOL with his unassuming, unpretentious, but hard-driving and intense personality. This chapter looks at Case as a human and AOL as a firm with humanity.

By all accounts, a current net worth in the billions of dollars has left Steve Case little changed. His house in the suburbs of Northern Virginia is unostentatious (e.g., no pool or tennis court). He motors limo-less, preferring to drive his own SUV or VW bug (and rejecting the idea of a hired driver even on the day the AOL–Time Warner merger was announced). The view from his office takes in power lines and a Wal-Mart. His favored lunch remains a turkey sandwich and a bag of Sun Chips.[1] And, perhaps most important, he still spends lots of time "lurking all over the America Online universe as if he were an average user," according to *The Washington Post*, interacting with the just-plain-folks who by the millions form AOL's core constituency.[2]

Is it any wonder that most of those people can't help but want to like Case, root for AOL, and forgive the many transgressions of the CEO and his company?

STAMP THE WORKPLACE WITH YOUR HUMANITY

Steve Case is so much an everyman that he's still able to stroll suburban shopping malls without being recognized. What's more surprising than that is his claim to be quite happy with such circumstances: he says it allows him to go to a movie with his kids like other dads: "The ability to have a normal life is actually what I'm trying to preserve."[3]

What's still more surprising is he means it. "In my case, it really is about believing that there is work to be done to build a medium that we can be proud of," he says. "It's not about so-called power, or visibility, or stature. Those are things that I don't particularly enjoy."[4]

Why has Case's apparent great comfort with himself meant much to the improbable success of AOL? Because, the consensus holds, he's managed to mold a company remarkably free of the smug superiority that can so easily fell the high and mighty, thereby keeping himself and AOL in tune with the people they serve. An article in *The Washington Post* may best express how Case's unusual personality for a high-tech entrepreneur translates to AOL's enviable bottom line:

> "He is described as the technocrat politician more than the entrepreneur. This approach … may be better suited to long-term success, friends say. 'Other technology executives seem to have blinders on,' said George Vradenburg, AOL's general counsel. 'Steve has 360-degree vision. He integrates a lot of views when he's making decisions.' … James Kimsey, AOL's chairman emeritus and founder … added that Case is 'much more at home behind a keyboard than a podium.' "[5]

This is not to say that Case can't take the stage to fire up the troops when it's called for. *Time* magazine described his appearance before "a packed room of demoralized, worried employees" of CompuServe, shortly after AOL had acquired this once much-larger rival. After a rousing pep talk in which he donned a CompuServe-logo shirt, he left his new employees "laughing and cheering."[6]

KEEP PERSONAL LIMITATIONS FROM LIMITING THE ORGANIZATION

If it's your impression that it takes a dynamic, forceful, and charismatic management style to lead a modern company, allow Steve Case to dispel any such notions. Perhaps his most pronounced unleader-like trait – shyness – was first to emerge during his boyhood forays into enterprise with brother Dan. It was Dan who tended to assume the roles calling for face-to-face contact with customers. Steve, meanwhile, was apparently content to remain in the background, where he hatched the duo's various business ventures and handled marketing responsibilities.

Later, as Case gained experience in the adult world of work, particularly in his early days as head of AOL, other leader-like limitations came to the fore. In particular, he was said to lack the discipline required to bring employees together in pursuit of common goals. "Distant and taciturn, he has often allowed his subordinates to wander off on uncoordinated pursuits," says *The New York Times*, in a typical assessment.[7]

And Case's shyness for a time cost him AOL's top job. During the run-up to the company's 1992 IPO, when investment

STEVE CASE: GROWING UP ENTREPRENEURIAL[8]

- *Born:* August 21, 1958, in Honolulu, Hawaii.
- *Early years:* Case's childhood was pervasively American suburban – and entrepreneurial. Youthful ventures, almost always in partnership with brother Dan, included a lemonade stand, newspaper route, ad circular distribution, and Hawaii representation of a Swiss watch manufacturer that captured not one sale.
- *Family – then:* Born to native Hawaiian parents – dad a corporate lawyer and mom a teacher. Today, older brother Dan heads San Francisco investment bank Hambrecht & Quist, older sister Carin is a Santa Rosa, California, teacher, and younger brother Jeff is an insurance executive in San Francisco.
- *School:* BA in political science, 1980, from Williams College, Massachusetts.
- *Employment:* Started in marketing with Procter & Gamble (1980–82), where he unsuccessfully tried to sell the public on a bad idea – a moist tissue coated with hair conditioner – with the slogan "Towelette? You Bet!" Moved on to a post with PepsiCo's Pizza Hut unit (1982–83), where he was charged with recommending new pizza toppings and learned – in a way that would later influence his ceaseless drive to make AOL as simple as possible – that people want cheese, tomato sauce, and sometimes pepperoni. Unhappy with work he described as "all incremental rather than breaking new ground," he chucked it in the blink of an eye when given the chance to join online pioneer Control Video Corporation in 1983.
- *Family – today:* He lives in Fairfax, Virginia, with second wife Jean Villenueva (previously AOL's VP communications) and five young children. He has three children from an 11-year marriage to his college girlfriend that ended in divorce.

- *Social personality:* Generally described in neutral or unfavorable terms such as bland, distant, impersonal, something of a bore. Even more harshly, a business rival judges him "as cold as Spock on a bad day."[9]
- *Business personality:* Perhaps best encapsulated by Netscape founder and erstwhile Case subordinate Marc Andreessen as "half nerd and half marketing guy ... He's enough of a nerd to be really into online services, but he has all the marketing skills to understand how to make it work."[10]
- *Appearance:* Could disappear in a crowd of two. Says *Newsweek:* "He likes colorful Hawaiian shirts, but on Case, they somehow look like drab oxford cloth."[11]
- *Diversions:* In college, sang for two new-wave rock groups, produced concerts, and created a company that made a record album called "The Best of Williams." Today, goes online under any of several aliases to chat with AOL subscribers and surf the Net.
- *Dislike:* Discussion of his personal role in building the Internet or in significant AOL business moves, including acquisitions and alliances.

bankers warned that he lacked the schmoozing skills of an appealing front man, Case agreed to step down – in what turned out to be a temporary move – in favor of the more outgoing and polished Jim Kimsey.[12]

Case – to his great credit (and success and wealth) – also handled his other leadership shortcomings in a way very unlike most leaders: he faced them squarely and assembled a top team that possessed in spades the needed characteristics he lacked. His first shot at this misfired, when ex-Federal Express executive William Razzouk, hired in June 1996 to run day-to-day operations, departed under the all-purpose "other opportunities" charade after only four months on the job.[13] But Case then hit the bull's-eye by bringing in a member of his own board, MTV co-founder and Century 21 Real Estate CEO Bob Pittman.

Pittman's beneficial effects were soon evident within and outside the company. An AOL supplier's CEO, for example, says, "Dealing with AOL, you had the feeling of a bunch of kids playing at business. Pittman is their first adult supervision."[14]

Case faced his leadership shortcomings squarely and assembled a top team that possessed in spades the needed characteristics he lacked.

With Pittman and others in place who could compensate for Case's perceived shortcomings, the CEO still had to somehow cope with the shyness that simply can't be accommodated in the CEO of the US's largest new-media company. So Case attacked it with hard work and determination to make himself do what he's inclined to avoid, eventually earning credit for becoming "a prominent spokesman for AOL."[15]

Aside from that achievement, Case's unusual willingness to deal with his managerial flaws by bringing in those who would outshine him has served him and his company well. He's been able to largely remain true to his nature, which is not without its own benefits. *Newsweek*, for example, after noting that "Case is regarded as a bit of a stiff by reporters and other industry executives," added that employees see him "as imperturbable and intensely loyal. Turnover among top managers at AOL has been comparatively low."[16]

Similarly, *The Washington Post* reported in 1998 that Case:

> "… has been seen as a plodding, deliberate leader, more man-agement wonk than techie geek. In an industry whose best-known figures … are known as fiery control freaks, Case is a cool, consensus-building chief executive … 'Steve Case will never be mentioned with Bill Gates and Steve Jobs as a vision-ary or inventor,' said Paul Noglows, a technology industry analyst … 'But when our children read about the history of the Internet, they're going to be reading about Steve Case.' "[17]

BUILD A TOP TEAM THAT COVERS ALL BASES

A charge frequently leveled against some corporate CEOs, that he or she has hired a top team of "Mini-Me"s and yes-men, is unlikely to ever be heard by Steve Case. This is not to say Case's chief aides are at odds with the CEO or wish to take AOL in entirely different directions. Indeed, Case himself reports that his top aides are "people who had demonstrated track records in having built something and possessed the passion, persever-ance, and paranoia that we look for."[18] Numerous press accounts confirm that the tier of AOL executives who report directly to Case clearly shares his corporate vision and mission.

But these and other accounts also note that Case has assembled a top team with collective experience and talents that are su-perbly complementary. Case and his lieutenants fit together as precisely as pieces of a finely crafted jigsaw puzzle.

In president and COO Bob Pittman, Case found the executive who has exactly the sort of feet-on-the-ground feel for daily

A LEADER IN WAYS THAT LEADERSHIP MATTERS

Steve Case seems to fit no expert's notion of the conventional corporate leader. Yet he's repeatedly triumphed with the longest of odds against his company, led AOL to astounding growth and success, and won the respect and loyalty of employees from acquired CEOs to call center customer service reps. These excerpts from press reports comment on his rare leadership style and accomplishments.

- "[Case] is not the sort of guy ... who particularly likes to run a company with tens of thousands of employees, attend black-tie dinners, or schmooze with politicians. He'd rather be in front of his computer, thinking deep thoughts, firing off e-mails and otherwise living that wired life." – *The Washington Post*[19]

- " 'I'm younger than Bill Gates, but older than Marc Andreessen,' Case said ... 'Maybe I'm the average between those two, and therefore have the right point of view.' " – *Forbes*[20]

- "Even by the standards of the high-tech industry, Case is an unlikely corporate titan. In contrast to Gates, Malone, and other technology czars, he seems to have kept his ego in check." – *US News & World Report*[21]

- "... his employees had nicknamed him 'The Wall' because of the serene calm he projected in the face of even the most dire crisis." – *The National Post* (Canada)[22]

- "His office garb is aggressively casual: denim, polos, or Hawaiian shirts. Indeed, the juxtaposition of Case and Levin at the podium during last week's [merger announcement] press conference was downright odd. Few can remember the last time they saw Case wear a suit." – *US News & World Report*[23]

> • " 'Steve is very deceptive because he is so low-key and he certainly does not fit anyone's stereotype of what a hard-driving CEO should be like,' said Steven Rattner, an investment banker ... who advises America Online. 'But there is a quiet forcefulness to him ... that has made America Online what it has become today.' " – *The Washington Post*[24]

operations that mostly eludes the CEO. Investors considered that quality to be AOL's greatest need in 1996, before the company plucked Pittman from his less-than-fulfilling post as CEO of Century 21 Real Estate. "What AOL needed was someone who could shift investors' focus back to tomorrow's grand prospects," according to *Money* magazine. "Steve Case certainly had the vision to guide AOL as a business ... But AOL had to have another leader to complement him, someone who could work a room of Wall Street analysts and sell them on the service's potential. The board of directors found that person within its own ranks: outside director Robert Pittman."[25]

Case was unquestionably the brains behind the ease of use and strong sense of community that attracted the millions of subscribers who made AOL the runaway number one Internet service provider. But Pittman, according to *Fortune*, fulfilled the crying need for "someone who could finally translate all these customers into a real business." He did so in a number of ways, such as attacking costs. He negotiated with providers such as WorldCom to reduce AOL's cost of connect time down from 95 cents an hour to less than 50 cents an hour.[26]

The Wall Street Journal adds that Pittman proved his value by "bringing in new gushers of revenue by selling [AOL's] subscriber base to marketers and decreasing its reliance on subscription fees," but opines that Pittman may have yet to make his greatest contribution to AOL's success, stating:

> "... he is uniquely positioned to bridge the big gap between the old and new media worlds. While high-tech executives like Microsoft's Bill Gates stumbled trying to move into the media world and media executives like [Time Warner chief Gerald] Levin stumbled trying to move into high tech, Mr. Pittman is the rare executive who has succeeded in both. And he already has a history with Time Warner, thanks to his earlier involvement in both the launch of MTV by Warner Communications and the operation of Time Warner's theme parks."[27]

Other members of AOL leadership contribute unique strengths to the company's "deep bench." Ted Leonsis has a gift for identifying what the public – particularly youth – will want in the way of hot new entertainment. Corporate development chief Miles Gilburne, *The New York Times* says, "concocted some of the world's most complex acquisition deals." And rising star Barry Schuler "runs most of the programming services and is spearheading the company's forays into the world of electronic devices beyond the PC."[28]

The unique flavor of the executive recipe in which ingredient-incumbents so ideally complement each other is perhaps best described by AOL board member and former Novell CEO Robert Frankenberg: "You can't talk to Ted [Leonsis] without talking about content. Steve [Case] is the one asking what the member experience is like. And Bob [Pittman] asks, 'How do we make money off this?' "[29]

GROW A CULTURE THAT SPURS PEAK PERFORMANCE

There is a series of direct lines, as certain and factual as those composing a family tree, that lead from the personality that Steve Case brought to the ill-fated, barely-online venture called Control Video in 1983 to the corporate culture of today's AOL, colossus of the Internet.

In those early days, possibly even beneath the level of his own conscious recognition, Case was discovering what works online and what doesn't through his trial-and-error efforts on behalf of Control Video and Quantum Computer Services. Case was learning with ferocity, "putting in workaholic hours," according to *The Washington Post*. The process was hardly without cost – it contributed to the break-up of his first marriage. But "he was officially in charge by 1991. That was the year Quantum … decided to make its offerings available to all systems. And America Online was born."[30]

Years later – and lasting right to the present – the palpable energy generated by experimentation, innovation, flubs, and victories is still what makes AOL tick. A 1996 look inside the company by *The Washington Post* revealed that:

> "AOL is, as it always was, a fascinating, seductive place with strange language patterns, curious rituals and a religious zeal that would make the Christian Coalition covetous. Its inhabitants, AOLiens, dwell on an isolated planet where the sun never rises and seasons pass unnoticed. For them, life online is the only way to live …

> "[Case's] mug is an all-American combination of baby face and door-to-door weariness. He would, in fact, like to sell his wares

THE TOP TEAM ON STEVE'S CASE[31]

- *Robert W. Pittman*, 46, is the son of a Mississippi preacher who assembled a diverse pre-AOL resume that includes service as NBC's top radio programmer by age 20, co-founding the MTV music video network (and developing its legendary "I want my MTV" ad campaign) for Warner–Amex cable, heading Warner Communications' Six Flags amusement park unit, and co-owning and operating Century 21 Real Estate – where he made AOL's first million-dollar ad buy and got the attention of Steve Case, who asked him to join AOL's board. He was hired as one of three AOL division chiefs, but quickly emerged as number two to Case.

- *Barry M. Schuler*, 46, heads AOL's interactive services group, overseeing the critical drive to extend AOL to cell phones, television set-top boxes, and other devices. Schuler is the rarity at AOL who is so common at other Internet firms: a true digit-head. He joined AOL in 1995 via acquisition of his firm, Medior, which developed interactive products and did design work for clients including AOL. Before co-founding that company, he'd also founded and/or headed a developer of Macintosh software and a high-tech marketing and communications company. Scorned by the Silicon Valley digerati he lived among when he sold to the "Kmart" of Internet companies, Schuler now holds AOL stock worth about $1 billion and is regarded as one of the most influential executives in his industry.

- *Theodore J. Leonsis*, 44, is almost invariably described as flamboyant and/or brash. He joined AOL in 1994, when the firm bought the company he founded, new-media marketing outfit Redgate Communications. Put in charge of AOL Studios to develop the all-important content that attracts and keeps those many millions of AOL subscribers, Leonsis suffered from being in a position that hemorrhaged money while not clearly accounting for significant revenue. Today he runs the ICQ instant messaging service and several other youth-oriented brands.

Avon-lady-style. 'I'm convinced,' he says, 'that if I went to everybody's house and spent an hour with them – explaining the service, answering their questions – nobody would quit.'"[32]

More recently, *The New York Times* reported that AOL, "to avoid becoming too bureaucratic and introverted … hopes to buy some of the most creative start-ups."[33] The strategy appears to have worked.

> The palpable energy generated by experimentation, innovation, flubs, and victories is still what makes AOL tick.

And now, with the pending merger of AOL and the far more structured, some might say hidebound, Time Warner, AOL faces the greatest test of maintaining its winning corporate culture. A.G. Edwards analyst Michael A. Kupinski seems to think AOL's leadership is up to the task. "AOL has this tremendous management team that has a lot of vision," he told *The Washington Times*. "It sees the future in terms of the need to grow content. This merger with Time Warner gives AOL exactly what it needs to get to the next level."[34]

GIVE YOUR BUSINESS A HUMAN FACE

The personality of Steve Case has become the personality of AOL – and has carried the company to preeminence in the online world. There are important lessons for any current or future leader in the ways Case has managed to extend his humanity to and through his company:

- *Stamp the workplace with your humanity.* In the corporate world, Steve Case may be the best representative ever of an un-leader. His defining character traits are not those associated with a successful CEO – which may be exactly why those traits have proven so appealing to AOL employees and customers.

- *Keep personal limitations from limiting the organization.* Case appears able to confront his managerial shortcomings without letting his ego get in the way. He brings in aides who are strong where he is weak, and gives them the room they need to shine in ways Case himself could not.

- *Build a top team that covers all bases.* AOL's executive corps works as a team in the truest sense of what teamwork should accomplish. Their collective effectiveness is greater than the sum of its parts – a prime example of synergy in action that your firm may do well to emulate.

- *Grow a culture that spurs peak performance.* Within AOL, the drive and intensity of the CEO has been transmitted like a lightning bolt throughout the organization. Despite soaring growth of the company in size, success, and influence, the drive and enthusiasm of Steve Case in his earliest days with the company that became AOL appears undiminished – and able to survive the challenges ahead.

NOTES

1. Jared Sandberg, "Case Study," *Newsweek*, January 24, 2000.

2. Kara Swisher, "Steve Case Tries to Hold a Place Online," *The Washington Post*, August 27, 1995.

3. Jared Sandberg, "Case Study," *Newsweek*, January 24, 2000.

4. Thomas J. Neff and James M. Citrin, *Lessons from the Top: The Search for America's Best Business Leaders*, Currency-Doubleday, New York, 1999.

5. Mark Leibovich, "Steve Case Plods to the Vanguard of the Internet," *The Washington Post*, November 25, 1998.

6. Joshua Cooper Ramo, "How AOL Lost the Battles but Won the War," *Time*, September 22, 1997.

7. Saul Hansell, "Now, AOL Everywhere," *The New York Times*, July 4, 1999.

8. Compiled from numerous reports.

9. Jared Sandberg, "Case Study," *Newsweek* January 24, 2000.

10. Rajiv Chandrasekaran, "A Case of Timing, Knowledge," *The Washington Post*, January 11, 2000.

11. Jared Sandberg, "Case Study," *Newsweek*, January 24, 2000.

12. Jared Sandberg, "Case Study," *Newsweek*, January 24, 2000.

13. Marc Gunther, "The Internet Is Mr. Case's Neighborhood," *Fortune*, March 30, 1998.

14. Saul Hansell, "America Online's Triumvirate in Cyberspace," *The New York Times*, February 16, 1998.

15. Amy Cortese and Amy Barrett, "The Online World of Steve Case," *Business Week*, April 15, 1996.

16. Jared Sandberg, "Case Study," *Newsweek*, January 24, 2000.

17. Mark Leibovich, "Steve Case Plods to the Vanguard of the Internet," *The Washington Post*, November 25, 1998.

18. Thomas J. Neff and James M. Citrin, *Lessons from the Top: The Search for America's Best Business Leaders*, Currency-Doubleday, New York, 1999.

19. Rajiv Chandrasekaran, "A Case of Timing, Knowledge," *The Washington Post*, January 11, 2000.

20. Gene Koprowski, "AOL CEO Steve Case," *Forbes ASAP*, October 7, 1996.

21. Fred Vogelstein, "The Talented Mr. Case," *US News & World Report*, January 24, 2000.

22. David Akin, "The Winner's Case: Steve Case Has Overcome Many Setbacks," *The National Post*, November 25, 1998.

23. Fred Vogelstein, "The Talented Mr. Case," *US News & World Report*, January 24, 2000.

24. Kara Swisher, "Steve Case Tries to Hold a Place Online," *The Washington Post*, August 27, 1995.

25. John Helyar, "If You Want to Understand What's Happened to the Stock Market in the Past Three Years Just Look at America Online," *Money*, October 1999.

26. Marc Gunther, "The Internet Is Mr. Case's Neighborhood," *Fortune*, March 30, 1998.

27. Bruce Orwall and John Lippman, "Can Bob Pittman Make it All Click?" *The Wall Street Journal*, January 11, 2000.

28. Saul Hansell, "Now, AOL Everywhere," *The New York Times*, July 4, 1999.

29. Saul Hansell, "America Online's Triumvirate in Cyberspace," *The New York Times*, February 16, 1998.

30. Kara Swisher, "Steve Case Tries to Hold a Place Online," *The Washington Post*, August 27, 1995.

31. Compiled from numerous reports.

32. Linton Weeks, "America Online Bytes the Bullet," *The Washington Post*, October 1, 1996.

33. Saul Hansell, "Now, AOL Everywhere," *The New York Times*, July 4, 1999.

34. Timothy Burn, "Case Gets Last Laugh: AOL Grew From Humble Beginnings," *The Washington Times*, January 11, 2000.

Three

NEVER BE DISSUADED FROM PURSUING YOUR DREAM

IN THIS CHAPTER

If Steve Case's early-1990s vision of what AOL could become had *not* been realized, business-school case studies (no pun intended) might forever examine his "impossible dream" as the product of a slightly out-of-kilter Don Quixote-like mind. But he's proved the world wrong and himself right more spectacularly, perhaps, than any business leader before. In a young, struggling company, says AOL's first technology chief, Marc Seriff, "there needs to be somebody who believes no matter what … Steve believed from the first day that this was going to be a big deal."[1] He was right, of course. This chapter explores how the power of one person's belief in his vision of the future can lift a company to unprecedented success.

S teve Case's brother Dan, a technology-oriented investment banker, recalls introducing Steve in 1983 to the head of the struggling online services provider that eventually would evolve into AOL. "I thought the business was interesting, but I was not blown away," Dan recounts. "But I will never forget the look on Steve's face when he started talking about it all. He was so excited because he had finally found his place."[2]

And Steve would never be discouraged from believing that place was at the center of an information revolution – even though he would for years remain one of few people who'd even heard the first shots of that revolution. In AOL's early years, Case would lead the company through so many brushes with extinction that the firm would be called "the cockroach of cyberspace" for having survived against all odds.[3] In retrospect, it's clear the firm would have disappeared in the pages of corporate history had Steve Case believed even a little less fervently that his view of the future was on target.

GO WHERE NO ONE HAS GONE BEFORE

In business today, the leg up to be had by turning a great idea into a one-of-a-kind product or service is called "first-mover advantage." Considered broadly, we can look back and see first-mover advantage in great achievements – such as being first to fly solo across the Atlantic or to run a mile in less than four minutes.

But it's one thing to be Charles Lindbergh or Roger Bannister, and another to be Steve Case. The former two groundbreakers registered firsts that may have been thought unlikely by many people, but were at least generally conceivable by the human mind.

"Steve's known exactly what he wanted to do for longer than most people knew there were even those opportunities out there."
– Netscape co-founder Marc Andreessen

But Steve Case pictured a world in which people are interactively connected to each other via computers, televisions, phones, and other devices when few people even knew "interactive" as a word. He not only wanted to go, in the words of the *Star Trek* preamble, "where no one has gone before," he wanted to go where no one had conceived of before. As Marc Andreessen, no slouch as a visionary himself in helping found Netscape, puts it: "Steve's known exactly what he wanted to do for longer than most people knew there were even those opportunities out there."[4]

He knew at least as early as 1980 – as he applied for his first post-college job with media companies such as Time Inc. – that a revolution in individualized, electronic communication was on its way. (He was influenced by futurist Alvin Toffler's *The Third Wave*, a best-seller that discussed a coming shift from an industrial to an information-based economy.)[5] Only a few years later, he recounted for *The Washington Post*, Case knew the weapon that would spark the revolution would be the personal computer:

> "In the early 1980s, I was working in Wichita, Kansas, for PepsiCo. I bought a personal computer – a Kaypro CP/M computer – and tried to hook it up with a modem. It was a very rudimentary set-up. The first modem didn't work, and I had to order another one. It was all very painful and time-consuming, but I could glimpse the future. There was something magical about being able to dial out to the world from Wichita."[6]

If you have any memory of those Jurassic days of the PC and its agonizingly slow 300-baud link to the world beyond, you know the feeling expressed in *Fortune*'s assertion that, "Others would have quit. Case was entranced." He recalls thinking, "The ability to … connect with people all over the world – how could that not, over time, be a huge business?"[7] Yes, how not, we can readily agree today. But Case was virtually alone in his vision back then – or at least alone in being willing to stake his career on it – and would be laughed at and scorned for years to come.

If you believe in first-mover advantage – as prominent thinkers about business increasingly do in our speeded-up global economy – a visionary such as Case gains the edge as a first-and-only mover. It's an edge he apparently wishes to maintain, according to a recent assessment of AOL's possible future in *US News & World Report*. The AOL–Time Warner merger, the magazine holds, indicates Case's intention "to change the whole definition of [online] content. In many ways, the Internet is at a stage of development similar to television in the early days. In the late 1940s and early 1950s, television producers relied on radio stars like Jack Benny and George Burns to bring their 'content' onto television. But at first, the stars just reproduced what they were doing on radio. They didn't customize their content to take full advantage of the new visual medium. That took time."[8]

And to bring an equivalent transformation to the Net, perhaps, Case took Time Warner.

PURSUE YOUR PASSION RELENTLESSLY

It's easy to look at Steve Case today and wish to be a business leader like him. Here's the CEO who's got it all: fame, fortune, and a place in business history.

It's easy to forget that Case's current lofty position is hardly one he's accustomed to – that he's far more familiar with doubt and derision than with adulation. How many people have sufficient dedication to an idea, and imperviousness to insult, to stick with a commercial concept judged unworkable by many, and loony by most of the rest?

Recounting his early years at AOL for authors of the book *Lessons From the Top*, Case said, "perseverance is important, particularly in new industries, because there are many times where the so-called smart thing may be to throw up your hands and quit because it's hard, or you've hit a brick wall."[9]

Time magazine reminds us that, "Odds are, if you're a visionary, most of your years have been a struggle to get others to see what is so apparent to you ... Case imagined a world where ordinary folk ... would find real utility in connected computers. Almost everyone considered that a perfectly ridiculous idea."[10]

Yes, "almost everyone" abandoned that stance some time ago, but it was replaced by one in which "Steve Case was considered a bit of a fool by the New York kingpins of media and Silicon Valley's technology czars," as *The Wall Street Journal* put it. "And why not? In 1995, his company was in serious trouble ... Most of the high-tech elite had written off America Online Inc. Nonetheless ... Mr Case predicted to anyone who would listen that AOL would become one of the most powerful companies of the 21st century ... It seemed like an arrogant, even crazy, boast at the time. But Mr Case never wavered from his vision."[11]

> "Case imagined a world where ordinary folk ... would find real utility in connected computers. Almost everyone considered that a perfectly ridiculous idea."
> – *Time*

UUNet CEO John W. Sidgmore, who's known Case since 1994, says Case has had "a religious, long-term vision of what he was building," that reflected more than the desire for business success. "He genuinely likes being online. He really believes in the product he's pitching."[12]

Case believes, in other words, with a passion – an ingredient for business success that only recently is being recognized as not merely important, but essential. "Passion is a heart-driven approach," says consultant Richard Chang, author of *The Passion Plan: A Step-by-Step Guide to Discovering, Developing, and Living Your Passion*. We're accustomed to a "head-driven approach" in

CASE CLOSED: A DARING "NO" TO BILL GATES[13]

In May 1993, Steve Case found that his dream of helping to bring interconnectivity to the world was more powerful than all the facts, logic, and cold rationality he could muster. He could take the over-whelmingly more reasonable route of choosing to sell AOL to Microsoft. Or he could elect to keep his company independent, and thereby add the threat of direct competition from Microsoft to a laundry list of reasons that AOL had little prospect of becoming any more than a minor player in making the Internet – if it survived at all. Case chucked the sensible alternative by saying "no" to Bill Gates.

Case and Gates met face-to-face for the first time on May 11 1993, at Microsoft headquarters. The meeting was impromptu and with-out a planned agenda; Case's reason for traveling to the Pacific Northwest had been a meeting that morning with Microsoft co-founder Paul Allen, by then a private investor who'd recently been buying AOL stock with a possible takeover in mind. Case had brashly turned down peaceful accommodation of billionaire Allen, and now heard these first words ever from the Gates half of Microsoft's found-ing duo: "I can buy 20 percent of you, or I can buy all of you. Or I can go into this business myself and bury you."

Case and his top aides were noncommittal, returning to their Vir-ginia headquarters to take up the matter of selling with AOL's board. "AOL needed to decide whether to enter into discussions with [Gates] or go it alone," *The Wall Street Journal* later recounted. "It was a stark choice because AOL had only 250,000 subscribers, and pushing past CompuServe and Prodigy was going to take all the re-sources that the company could muster. Even with strong buzz about the potential for AOL, the company's growth remained sluggish."

The directors split into two factions, with Case heading the anti-sale contingent. "I recognized that if we sold, everyone would make a bunch of money and we could all just go off," he says. "So the question was: Did we want to be an also-ran?" The *Journal* says Case considered negotiations "a mistake that they would regret for the rest of their lives. AOL was not even into Act I yet, [Case]thought."

When the board was polled, Case's no-sale position was upheld by a margin of one director. Perhaps a statement by director Doug Peabody, a venture capitalist, won the day: "Do we want to be a footnote on Bill Gates's resume, or do we want to be the king of the online industry?" he had asked those in the room. "We have constantly undervalued ourselves and we have gotten this far. Now it's too late to turn back."

our work lives, Chang asserts – which certainly has its place in planning, reasoning, and rationalizing, he says. "But it's important to start with the heart, to know what really matters to you and what brings you happiness."[14]

That Case knew what mattered to him two decades ago – when his passion was for an interconnected world that then had no practical means of interconnection – is remarkable in retrospect. "It is really hard to have such a bold vision in the technology industry. You really needed to have vision in the early 1980s to comprehend what the Internet could do," says Bobbie Kilberg, who heads the technology council that serves AOL's headquarters area. "Steve Case had the vision and enough determination to stick with it through the good times and the bad. What he has done is extraordinary."[15]

BELIEVE WHAT YOU KNOW MORE THAN WHAT YOU'RE TOLD

With the incessant drumbeat of critics' harsh judgments of virtually his every strategic move and management decision, it's a wonder that Steve Case didn't crack, as in an East vs. West spy novel, blurting out his willingness to say AOL is doomed if he could just be freed of the continuous drip-drip-drip of disapproving lectures.

Case has at last persuaded some observers that AOL has accomplished something remarkable over the past ten years. For example, analyst Lise Buyer of CS First Boston, appearing on CNN "Moneyline," says, "There have been a couple of Internet companies that basically have been lucky. AOL is not one of them. I actually credit this to Steve Case – he believed in what he was doing when no one else believed."[16]

Technology editor and author Anthony B. Perkins 'fesses up to past doubts about AOL in admitting that, "Steve Case is a strategic genius with a capital G. Back in the mid-1990s – when Netscape was on its way up, when Microsoft had AOL in its cross hairs and was bragging about launching its own proprietary online service, the Microsoft Network – all of us in Silicon Valley were calling AOL toast."[17]

One of the many amazing aspects of the continuing clash between Case's belief in what he's doing and the world's certainty that he's wrong is that Case has never pulled a retrospective Al Gore-ism ("I took the initiative in creating the Internet"). Instead, he has espoused his core business beliefs – publicly and consistently – from Day One of his career. *Wall Street Journal* technology columnist Walter S. Mossberg recently recalled his first meeting with Case, when "his upstart online service, America Online, had just 200,000 members – about one percent of today's total – and it was a distant third in its industry. Yet he looked me in the eye that day in 1992 and swore that AOL would someday be a huge media company … I recommended the largely unknown AOL to my readers … But I still didn't believe his bold prediction."[18]

On another occasion, Mossberg attributed the scorn for AOL among "techies" to their view of the company "as pedestrian and philistine. They see it as the gateway through which the unwashed masses have flooded onto the Internet to pollute a medium they once called their own."[19]

And it seems clear that no level or amount of success will ever convince all critics that what Steve believes seems to be proven time and again to be dead on-target. Writing in *The Wall Street Journal* in 1997, for example, *FEED* magazine founder and editor Stefanie Syman dismissed AOL's past success, asserting it "doesn't say much about the future":

> "[AOL] was a distant third in its industry. Yet [Case] looked me in the eye that day in 1992 and swore that AOL would someday be a huge media company."
> – *Wall Street Journal* columnist Walter S. Mossberg

"[M]any Americans who cut their teeth on AOL now find it kludgy and precious … Proprietary on-line services have lost their edge with customers, who need quick, reliable e-mail and easy access to the Web … AOL has touted features like chat 'rooms' and bulletin boards … Yet, the Web now supports these

tools ... And AOL's other advantage, ease of use, is also di-
minishing: Besides ever-proliferating ISPs with ready-made
software like C-Net's Snap Online, big players like Bell Atlantic will soon enter the fray ... [T]he types of devices that connect
to the Web multiply. So does AOL's competition ... AOL seems
to assume, arrogantly, that cash and marketing might are
enough."[20]

In 1996, one year before these words appeared in print, Steve
Case told *Forbes* magazine, "This is going to be a mass market.
It is going to embrace tens of millions of customers."[21]

On New Year's Day 2000, AOL subscribers – for the flagship
online service alone – topped 20 million, a gain of 11 million
since Syman's forecast of AOL's bleak prospects. What Steve
believes had again become real.

NEVER BE DISSUADED FROM PURSUING YOUR DREAM

Steve Case has known and maintained a laser-like focus on his
career mission for more than two decades. That in itself is no
mean accomplishment, but it rises to remarkable proportions
for having been achieved in spite of continual doubting, scorn,
and derision from virtually every supposed expert in the industry. If you think you can't go it alone in making your dream
a reality, here's a Case-in-point that it's possible if you:

- *Go where no one has gone before.* Innovation and value-creation
  happen so fast today that a me-too business can't reasonably
  expect long-term success. Whether you call it pushing the
  envelope, thinking outside the box, or plain old creativity –

you've got to latch on to something that hasn't been done (and perhaps has been judged impossible to do) and make it happen.

- *Pursue your passion relentlessly.* Business history is laden with examples of the entrepreneur plugging away in the face of universal doubt and even outright derision. But the Case example, thanks to the global reach of today's mass media, may top them all for relentless pursuit of a business vision that others see as business fantasy. The AOL success story is the business world's embodiment of perseverance.

- *Believe what you know more than what you're told.* The triumph of Steve Case's dream may demonstrate that the bolder a business vision is, the more it will be attacked by critics and naysayers. Hanging on to core beliefs in the face of torrents of doubt is essential to making your dream real.

NOTES

1. Marc Gunther, "The Internet Is Mr. Case's Neighborhood," *Fortune*, March 30, 1998.

2. Kara Swisher, "Steve Case Tries to Hold a Place Online," *The Washington Post*, August 27,1995.

3. Fred Vogelstein, "The Talented Mr. Case," *US News & World Report*, January 24, 2000.

4. Rajiv Chandrasekaran, "A Case of Timing, Knowledge," *The Washington Post*, January 11, 2000.

5. Kara Swisher, "Steve Case Tries to Hold a Place Online," *The Washington Post*, August 27, 1995.

6. Daniel Southerland, "America Online's Rapid Rise," *The Washington Post*, November 8, 1993.

7. Marc Gunther, "The Internet Is Mr. Case's Neighborhood," *Fortune*, March 30, 1998.

8. William J. Holstein, *et al.* "You've Got a Deal!" *US News & World Report*, January 24, 2000.

9. Thomas J. Neff and James M. Citrin, *Lessons from the Top: The Search for America's Best Business Leaders*, Currency-Doubleday, New York, 1999.

10. Joshua Cooper Ramo, "How AOL Lost the Battles but Won the War," *Time*, September 22, 1997.

11. Kara Swisher, "How Steve Case Morphed Into a Media Mogul," *The Wall Street Journal*, January 11, 2000.

12. Rajiv Chandrasekaran, "A Case of Timing, Knowledge," *The Washington Post*, January 11, 2000.

13. Kara Swisher, "Steve Case Tries to Hold a Place Online," *The Washington Post*, August 27, 1995; Kara Swisher, "When Bill Met Steve: A Showdown That Shaped AOL," *The Wall Street Journal*, June 22, 1998.

14. Author interview.

15. Timothy Burn, "Case Gets Last Laugh: AOL Grew From Humble Beginnings," *The Washington Times*, January 11, 2000.

16. CNN television network, "Moneyline News Hour," December 30, 1999.

17. Anthony B. Perkins, "AOL Beats the Odds – Again," *The Wall Street Journal*, January 12, 2000.

18. Walter S. Mossberg, "Will the New AOL Still Serve User Needs?" *The Wall Street Journal*, January 20, 2000.

19. Walter S. Mossberg, "If the Techies Hate the AOL–Netscape Deal, It Must Be Good for Us," *The Wall Street Journal*, December 3, 1998.

20. Stefanie Syman, "Is America Online a Leviathan or a Dinosaur?" *The Wall Street Journal*, September 15, 1997.

21. Gene Koprowski, "AOL CEO Steve Case," *Forbes ASAP*, October 7, 1996.

Four

KISS!

IN THIS CHAPTER

It's remarkable enough that Steve Case understood – probably earlier and more clearly than any other online industry executive – that what most people would want most was simplicity in gaining access to the interconnected world. More remarkable is that he successfully resisted pressures from every direction to abandon simplicity, jazz up his product, win the praise of his peers – and slowly but inevitably lose the key advantage that AOL rode to the pinnacle of the Internet. To the contrary, Case and his top team are vocally and demonstrably committed to making AOL even simpler to use than it is today. In this chapter, learn how Steve Case discovered that simplicity would be the key to success, kept the faith that he had a winning vision, and extended the drive to be simpler throughout his company.

KISS – "Keep it simple, stupid" – is far easier said than done. Most of us know simple is better and have every wish to keep things that way. But most of us, it seems, are inclined to form a notion of what's simple from our perspective as experts about the products or services we sell. What's understandable and easy for us may seem formidable to the average customer.

The genius of Steve Case is, in part, his ability to resist reflecting how brainy, cool, and leading-edge he is by building techno-wizardry into AOL offerings. He's paid for his insight and obstinacy by suffering the slings and arrows of countless Silicon Valley whiz kids, digit-heads, and techies – and cashed in by succeeding on a scale the critics probably couldn't even have imagined.

GRAB ON AND HANG TIGHT TO SIMPLICITY

To get to the idea of simplicity, Steve Case took the path of complexity and frustration. The instruments of his enlightenment, back in the early 1980s, were a footlocker-like Kaypro computer, a snail's-pace 300-baud modem, and a primitive online service called the Source. The cost, complexity, and unreliability of combining these elements to gain access to an extremely limited world of online information could – and did – discourage all but the most dedicated and fanatical of users – of whom Case was one. He looks back at those days by remarking, "It wasn't a great leap of faith to think that if you made it affordable and easy to use, people would want it."[1]

> "[Case's] story is a lesson in what a very smart man with a simple vision can do – if he isn't thrown off by fads and mockery and the usual demands of vanity and ego."
> – *Newsweek*

Case's ability even then to see the commercial potential of simplicity was probably aided by his then-brief work career. Having attempted unsuccessfully to fire up a needlessly complex wipe-on hair product for Procter & Gamble, then moved on to evaluating the market potential of exotic new pizza toppings for Pizza Hut, Case was exposed to two hints that simple is better. Consumers think fingers work fine in their hair, and they like pizza best when it's got little more than tomato sauce and cheese.

Tougher than recognizing the merits of simplicity is sticking with it. *Newsweek* observes that Case "seems guided by a gyroscope, an internal compass. His story is a lesson in what a very smart man with a simple vision can do – if he isn't thrown off by fads and mockery and the usual demands of vanity and ego."[2] That's a catalog of formidable foes that has derailed more than a few high-and-mighty business leaders, including would-be major players in the world of new media – chiefs of giants such as IBM and AT&T among them.

An object lesson in staying true to simplicity is revealed in AOL's 1999 release of new Windows software, version 5.0. AOL "has achieved primacy with an admirable focus on simplicity and clarity," according to a *Wall Street Journal* evaluation of the upgrade. "With all that success, however, has come a predicament. AOL needs to innovate, but it fears it can't change things too much lest it offend its members. So the giant of cyberspace moves cautiously."[3] The review proceeded to criticize such 5.0 features as the requirement "to go two levels down to find your personal stock quotes, or news headlines on topics you follow, or scores for your favorite sports teams. Services like 'My Yahoo' place these all right up front, where you can find them at a glance ... [T]hese sorts of more sophisticated features add value even for casual, nontechnical users."[4]

Perhaps so, but that perceived shortcoming went unnoted by a *New York Times* piece saying version 5.0 "maintains AOL's traditional emphasis on ease of use instead of jazzy, cutting-edge innovation, but it does add a handful of new features intended to appeal to a Norman Rockwell audience."[5]

The difference in these remarks provides a glimpse of what is most likely only the tip of the veritable iceberg of considerations surrounding the determination of what's simple and what isn't in the collective mind of millions of people of all ages, cultures, incomes, education levels, and online savvy – or lack

THE UN-TECHNOLOGY COMPANY

AOL has gotten where it is today by being in technology but not *of* technology. Steve Case is reported to have said that his least favorite college course was computer programming.[6] Similarly, Number Two man Bob Pittman is said to pride himself on being a non-techie, claiming instead, "I understand consumers."[7] Some comment on AOL's actual place in (or out of) technology:

- "We always said that we viewed AOL as being about the Internet and a whole lot more, and less about the technology and more about the experience." – Steve Case, on National Public Radio's "All Things Considered," December 5th, 1996[8]
- "What makes AOL a great steward for Netscape's technological crown jewels is the fact that it isn't primarily a technology company. Instead, AOL is a service company focused on providing consumers with content, commerce, and online communities of interest – and then marketing those things like mad." – *The Wall Street Journal*, December 3rd, 1998[9]
- "Pittman 'really clarified that we were a consumer product and not a technology,' says [AOL's Barry] Schuler." – *The Wall Street Journal*, March 19th, 1999[10]

of it. That AOL has unquestionably managed to stay simple *and* keep adding customers in the face of such considerations indicates a level of tenacity in Case and his company that others must admire and emulate.

MAKE YOUR PRODUCT WORK "JUST WELL ENOUGH"

The two reviews of AOL's version 5.0 – split as they are between acclaim and mild criticisms – illustrate how precisely AOL manages, in so many ways, to deliver to customers the services they want when they want them, but stop short of providing too much. "Case designed AOL for the rest of us," *Fortune* observes. "And it works, just well enough."[11]

Well enough, in particular, to provide the simplest communications by e-mail and in chat rooms – the two services Case was smart enough to recognize would become, and remain, by far the most popular among by far the majority of average folks, who don't need or even particularly want instant access to the last hour's trading volume in shares of EgoMania.com. "[W]herever it goes, America Online's focus is on fostering interest-based communities online ... the service's members spend 60 percent of their time communicating with one another," *The New York Times* noted in 1995. AOL VP Kathy Ryan said, "This medium is about participation, and not just a place to find information and download bits."[12]

> "[T]echnology observers lampooned AOL as the 'Internet on training wheels' ... [but] the easy-to-navigate AOL grew ever more popular with ordinary computer users."
> – *The Washington Post*

Ryan was unabashedly relaying a Steve Case mantra that long pre-dated her statement. *The Washington Post* recounts Case's bold "early bet to make his service markedly different from CompuServe and Prodigy, then the big dogs of the online world. Instead of the tech focus of CompuServe or the electronic shopping-oriented Prodigy, AOL would concentrate on making its service easy to use and promoting user interaction through chat rooms and message boards. It was a hit."

Rather, it was a hit with subscribers. Meanwhile "some technology observers lampooned AOL as the 'Internet on training wheels' and suggested that [services] such as AT&T's WorldNet … or EarthLink would put the company out of business, [but] the easy-to-navigate AOL grew ever more popular with ordinary computer users."[13]

Consider how daring and different it is, in any business, to refuse to play the "me-too" game of matching competitors' every move – particularly when you're the runt among those in the fray. AOL's brilliance was perhaps exceeded only by its audacity, as Case deliberately chose not to follow the leaders. The company, *Newsweek* points out:

> "… realized that what kept its users bound to the service was not stuff like sports or weather – you could get that anywhere on the Internet – but the information and interaction that its users themselves generated. By hosting hundreds of chat rooms, sponsoring the most popular instant message service on the globe and giving granny an e-mail address that she'd never figure out how to change, AOL kept its audience and saw growth accelerated by the Network Effect (the more people who sign up, the more valuable the service becomes)."[14]

That network effect is largely triggered by Case's brilliance in building an AOL that works just well enough to stand out clearly

as the least intimidating Internet service provider, thereby grab-
bing the greatest share of online "newbies" ("granny" among
them), and retaining them indefinitely because they never learn
to do much more than exchange e-mail, or most of their friends
and relatives are on AOL, or they'd switch to a hipper or more
extensive service but it isn't worth the bother to make it happen.

And what have competitors done in response to AOL's "laser-
like focus on average consumers and the simplicity and clarity
they seek"? Walter Mossberg contends they've "typically offered
users a complicated setup process and little guidance in navi-
gating the Net. One key difference has been that AOL's service
comes in the form of a single piece of software … The typical
ISP offers separate browsers, e-mail programs and chat software. The result is a more confusing offering, at least for novices
and casual users."[15]

This is why Mossberg reacts to the AOL–Time Warner merger
announcement as, in general, "a good thing for mainstream
Web surfers." He notes that AOL "has shrugged off the scorn
of the techies, refused to indulge in complex bells and whistles,
and delivered online community and content that everybody
can use. This history stands in stark contrast to the track record
of Microsoft and AT&T, which were once expected to swamp
AOL but couldn't escape their techie roots."[16]

FOCUS ON SERVING "THE REST OF US"

AOL leads its industry because it refuses to think like its industry. The need to do so seems obvious enough; that's why

companies say they're "customer-centric" and spend like mad on customer surveys and focus groups.

So it's curious that precious few companies, AOL among them, are cited time and again for being responsive to customers, while all the others keep studying these few – as if to discover a secret formula. Steve Case certainly seems surprised that anyone would have to dig to learn what obscure magic propelled his company's ascent. In 1996, *Business Week* reported, "There's nothing visionary about AOL, [Case] submits. Its success results from simply paying better attention to what consumers want than technology-obsessed rivals do. 'The industry pundits were out of touch with consumers. That was a huge mistake,' says Case."[17] Three years later, Case again said the basis of AOL's success is easily accessible to anyone: "Our strategy has always been crystal clear," he told *The San Francisco Chronicle*. "Consumers want a central location where they can find good content. And they want someone to make it easy for them."[18]

In other words, we're not talking rocket science, but uncomplicated, easily observable consumer behavior. So, "while others engaged in strategy *du jour*, AOL remained steady and plowed ahead with the same game plan. For more than a decade, Case has focused on building an audience by offering an easy-to-use Internet service for the rest of us."[19]

The implication that AOL couldn't go far wrong if it learned what techies want and did the opposite is made clear in this unqualified assertion by *The Wall Street Journal*: "Anything that horrifies Silicon snobs must be good for the rest of us."[20]

SIMPLY SAID, "YOU'VE GOT PICTURES"[21]

The genius of AOL-style simplicity is vividly displayed in the "You've Got Pictures" service the company introduced jointly with Kodak in late 1999.

The service is designed to allow AOL subscribers to toss the crumbling shoeboxes and forget all those partly-filled, static-laden, drugstore photo albums – and instead store their photos in online digital albums that can be fired at light speed to anyone with e-mail and appropriate software – AOL subscriber or not.

Like other AOL enhancements for subscribers, "You've Got Pictures," is aimed for easy use even by those of us whose snapshots routinely lop off the tops of subjects' heads. (Even AOL can't cure us of this.) When film is delivered for processing, the user simply checks an AOL box on the envelope and pays about $6 extra. The processor uploads the photos to AOL (and still provides the customary "hard copy" prints). When the subscriber next logs onto AOL, that same chirpy "You've got mail!" voice intones, "You've got pictures!"

Not only can the photos be downloaded and shared with others, but reprints can be ordered online, as can applications of selected pictures on products such as coffee mugs and tee-shirts.

The service does nothing more than what others have previously provided via the Web, *The Wall Street Journal* observes, "but AOL's presentation and integration of this one are much more appealing." AOL's special brand of simplicity wins again.

SUFFUSE THE ORGANIZATION WITH SIMPLICITY

Steve Case is a vision-and-mission sort of leader, not a detail-oriented, hands-on kind of executive who gets his people organized and aimed toward common goals. Result: Although he clearly saw, early in AOL's existence, that simplicity is what most consumers would most want from online service, he had no complementary vision for structuring the organization needed to achieve his overarching goals.

To Case's credit (*as discussed in Chapter 2*), he recognized his managerial shortcomings and has not been too proud to bring in subordinates whose strengths compensate for his weaknesses and allow them to shine where he comes up short. Thus, most importantly, second-in-command Bob Pittman fully bought into Case's dedication to simplicity and extended it in both inventive and mundane ways to every corner of AOL operations.

> Case "literally wanted to make something his mother could use easily."
> – AOL executive Barry Schuler

For example, "Pittman has in recent years been the executive who brought operational sense to Mr. Case's sprawling vision," says *The Wall Street Journal*.[22] The most dramatic illustration of this may be Pittman's reining in of AOL's incredibly high marketing costs, which for years were fueled mostly by the company's famous "carpet-bombing" strategy of distributing free-trial computer diskettes by the millions (*discussed in Chapter 8*). Pittman is given credit for recognizing that AOL's need to cover the earth in disks had arisen from its relative obscurity and last-place standing among the nationwide online services. With those conditions in its past, the company could more precisely target its marketing.

At about the same time, Pittman recognized that AOL's primary advertising slogan – which had been, "The future, available now" – should reflect the simplicity that most attracted its new subscribers. So he introduced a campaign based on, "So easy, no wonder it's No. 1."[23]

Pittman also brought spending controls to AOL's internal operations. Costs within the company had never gotten out of hand, as there was no money to spend in the early years and Case seems singularly uninterested in any of the costly perks that so many other CEOs somehow find indispensable to running their companies. (Example: AOL had fractional ownership of one plane when the planned merger with Time Warner was announced, while the partner possessed four aircraft outright.[24]) But low costs aren't necessarily controlled costs, and seem not to be a consideration that registers on Case's personal radar screen. It therefore was left to Pittman to impose management.

Barry Schuler, who heads AOL's interactive services unit, is perhaps the company's most unlikely top executive to extend simplicity, being a virtual card-carrying member of the Silicon Valley digit-head elite who seem to stay alive by breathing and heaping scorn on AOL. Schuler came to AOL via acquisition of his company, Medior, which was also courted by other prospective buyers. In a move by which Schuler would lose employees, associates, and supposed friends, he elected to become part of AOL because Case "literally wanted to make something his mother could use easily."[25]

Both Schuler and Pittman are cited by name in press accounts reporting their determination – and Case's – to make AOL even more user friendly. "We have got to make it easier still, and that will be spurred by using more sophisticated technology," Schuler says. "We're all going to hit the wall eventually until every part of the process is completely simple."[26]

Case and Pittman, according to *Time* magazine, "hope to capture the mindless simplicity of a television: on, off, a channel tuner." The impetus is not only attracting new subscribers, but making further significant cost cuts, as the company employs several thousand people who do nothing more than take calls from customers who can't make something work. (Often, it's some aspect of accessing AOL unrelated to the company's service. Turning on the computer is still a stumbling block for some callers.) "The customers keep us from kidding ourselves," says Pittman.[27]

Case views AOL's corps of customer service reps as "proof" of the need to maintain the drive toward simplicity. Neither he nor his top team will rest, apparently, until everyone sees AOL as simple.

KISS!

It seems nothing could be simpler than to deliver the simplicity customers crave, yet more corporate leaders fail in the effort than succeed. Steve Case and AOL have succeeded – spectacularly so – by focusing on simplicity in these ways:

- *Grab and hang tight to simplicity.* Steve Case has been almost alone among technology industry leaders in understanding from Day One that most people most want their online experience to be like their pizza toppings and everything else they buy: simple. And he's been even more exceptional in hewing to the simplicity credo as AOL has become ever-larger and more successful. His is the path less taken, but a path that can probably lead to as great a success for you as it did for him.

- *Make your product work "just well enough."* Sure, you're as familiar with your products and services as you are with your right hand. But does being comfortable with something necessarily mean you'll like it even more if you jazz it up with some added fancy features? The simplicity of a mousetrap can be what makes it a better mousetrap, as AOL has more decisively shown than any other company of the information age.

- *Focus on serving "the rest of us."* Most managers of high-tech companies may indeed act as if earth ends at the edges of Silicon Valley. But they're hardly alone in their corporate myopia: Business blunders and miscalculations indicate how easy it is to manage as if the world includes only the people we work with every day – whose notion of simple can be complex for everyone else. AOL has avoided limited vision like few firms before, showing what companies can gain by delivering simplicity as customers define it.

- *Suffuse the organization with simplicity.* Companies have plenty to gain by striving for simplicity in more than just their products and services. AOL has gained from lean operations, reasonable controls, and a never-ending quest for still-greater simplicity that extends throughout the organization.

NOTES

1. Fred Vogelstein, "The Talented Mr. Case," *US News & World Report*, January 24, 2000.

2. Jared Sandberg, "Case Study," *Newsweek*, January 24, 2000.

3. Walter S. Mossberg, "Treading Cautiously, AOL Adds Photos and Other New Tricks," *The Wall Street Journal*, October 7, 1999.

4. Walter S. Mossberg, "Treading Cautiously, AOL Adds Photos and Other New Tricks," *The Wall Street Journal*, October 7, 1999.

5. Peter H. Lewis, "Another Makeover for AOL," *The New York Times*, October 7, 1999.

6. Rajiv Chandrasekaran, "A Case of Timing, Knowledge," *The Washington Post*, January 11, 2000.

7. Bruce Orwall and John Lippman, "Can Bob Pittman Make it All Click?" *The Wall Street Journal*, January 11, 2000.

8. National Public Radio, "All Things Considered," December 5, 1996.

9. Walter S. Mossberg, "If the Techies Hate the AOL–Netscape Deal, It Must Be Good for Us," *The Wall Street Journal*, December 3, 1998.

10. Kara Swisher, "America Online's Next Frontier: Winning Respect in Silicon Valley," *The Wall Street Journal*, March 19, 1999.

11. Marc Gunther, "The Internet Is Mr. Case's Neighborhood," *Fortune*, March 30, 1998.

12. Steve Lohr, "Steve Case at a Crossroad," *The New York Times*, August 14, 1995.

13. Rajiv Chandrasekaran, "A Case of Timing, Knowledge," *The Washington Post*, January 11, 2000.

14. Steven Levy, "The Two Big Bets," *Newsweek*, January 24, 2000.

15. Walter S. Mossberg, "Earthlink Comes Close to AOL in Ease of Use but Needs to Do More," *The Wall Street Journal*, December 9, 1999.

16. Walter S. Mossberg, "Will the New AOL Still Serve User Needs?" *The Wall Street Journal*, January 20, 2000.

17. Amy Cortese and Amy Barrett, "The Online World of Steve Case," *Business Week*, April 15, 1996.

18. Jon Swartz, "Case Study – A Look at Mr. America Online," *The San Francisco Chronicle*, February 22, 1999.

19. Jon Swartz, "Case Study – A Look at Mr. America Online," *The San Francisco Chronicle*, February 22, 1999.

20. Walter S. Mossberg, "If the Techies Hate the AOL–Netscape Deal, It Must Be Good for Us," *The Wall Street Journal*, December 3, 1998.

21. Walter S. Mossberg, "Treading Cautiously, AOL Adds Photos and Other New Tricks," *The Wall Street Journal*, October 7, 1999; Peter H. Lewis, "Another Makeover for AOL," *The New York Times*, October 7, 1999.

22. Bruce Orwall and John Lippman, "Can Bob Pittman Make it All Click?" *The Wall Street Journal*, January 11, 2000.

23. Saul Hansell, "America Online's Triumvirate in Cyberspace," *The New York Times*, February 16, 1998.

24. Matt Murray, Nikhil Deogun, and Nick Wingfield, "Can Time Warner Click With AOL?" *The Wall Street Journal*, January 14, 2000.

25. Kara Swisher, "America Online's Next Frontier: Winning Respect in Silicon Valley," *The Wall Street Journal*, March 19, 1999.

26. Kara Swisher, "America Online's Next Frontier: Winning Respect in Silicon Valley," *The Wall Street Journal*, March 19, 1999.

27. Joshua Cooper Ramo, "How AOL Lost the Battles but Won the War," *Time*, September 22, 1997.

Five

IGNORE "IRRELEVANT" EXPERTS – CUSTOMERS RULE!

IN THIS CHAPTER

The best ballplayers know that every fan will express his opinion, but it's only the umpire's judgment that counts. Similarly, the best business executives recognize that their every decision will be critiqued by a host of experts, but only the customer's verdict shows up on the bottom line. Steve Case – thanks largely to his marketer's orientation – has understood from AOL's inception that consumers alone would determine the fate of his venture. So he has focused on them alone, delivered exactly the service they said they wanted, and reaped the rewards of doing so. Here are the ways Case and his aides built AOL for its customers.

On the day he announced the planned merger of his company with Time Warner, Steve Case brushed off the critics who'd hounded him for the past decade: "I never gave much heed to people who predicted our doom," he said. "They were irrelevant because they never understood what the customer wanted."[1]

Amazingly, though Case by dint of AOL's stupendous success has quelled the righteous blather of many critics, there are even today those who pontificate on Case's misapprehension of the online market and their correct view. Case gives them just as much credence as ever (none). He still is guided solely by customers – the people who hold the fate of any enterprise in their hands.

LET NO ONE BUT CUSTOMERS SHAPE YOUR BUSINESS

Steve Case and his company would have been much better liked by his Internet-firm peers, the media reps who cover the high-tech scene, and untold numbers of the coolest Web-heads if he'd run AOL the way they'd have liked. But uncool Case sticks stubbornly to a model that appeals to the masses – and, by the way, achieves that most un-Silicon status: profitability. For example, "[Microsoft's] difficulty with AOL is that it never quite seems to understand what makes AOL so strong," *The Economist* comments. "The answer is an unerring ability to understand the needs of consumers – something with which the computer industry has never much concerned itself."[2]

A mistake by others, of course, that has spectacularly rebounded to the greater glory of AOL. What Case learned, which others in his industry never bothered to look for, "was that the most important use of an online service was for people to communicate through e-mail, chat rooms, and, more recently, the hugely popular instant messages that users can send directly to their friends' screens," reports *The New York Times*.[3]

In retrospect, it appears that Case's literal and figurative distance from the center of the Internet world almost certainly aided his customer orientation. He is by natural inclination – and childhood experience – a marketer. No Jobs-ian, Gates-ian, Andreessen-ian long hours tinkering with computers in the garage for young Steve. He was lying awake in bed, pestering older brother Dan with a scheme-a-minute for selling some gee-whiz product everyone on the Hawaiian Islands would want. And Case's jobs in the embryonic online industry were with companies in the suburbs of Washington, DC, "light years from

Silicon Valley, [where] the world looks like a consumer marketplace, not a computer lab," notes *The Wall Street Journal*. "That's
why AOL is by far the most successful company on the Internet,
and the best-known online brand name."[4]

Case pairs distance from the digit-head's Mecca with closeness
to prospective customers. "[T]he center of gravity has to be the
consumer – what consumers want and how they want it," he
says, adding this bit of digital heresy: "If we look at it through
that prism, the Internet is an important piece
of that puzzle. But just a piece. There's
definitely an inside-the-Valley phe-
nomenon that is out of step with
reality."[5]

> "[T]he center of
> gravity has to be the
> consumer – what
> consumers want and
> how they want it."
> – Steve Case

What Case states politely can be
said with an edge by outsiders,
such as the principals of a small information services company in
Lexington, Massachusetts (again, far from Silicon Valley), whose article in the Internet-industry magazine
Upside asserted: "AOL's not interested in the code-spewing,
Usenet-posting, free-speech-shouting, cybersex-loving digerati
who are usually associated with the Internet. The 'technology
elite' are presumably the same cybersnobs who read *Upside* and
mock AOL for its hokey interface and its inability to synchro-
nize with the HTML- and Java-world technology."[6]

Perhaps those "cybersnobs" are most steamed at Case for making the computer and the online world it unlocked so easily
accessible to the average Joe and Jane. The digerati had once
been assumed by most people to have Merlin-like powers to
tap into the fearsome magic that computers could unlock –

until Case designed a service that said, "It's nothing more than ones and zeroes – and you can have it, too."

"The secret of Case is that he has figured out a way to make consumers like their computers," a Sun Microsystems executive contends. "Look at AOL's customer base – it's normal people, it's consumers … It was extremely arrogant of the high-tech industry to criticize that."[7]

HOW CASE GETS CLOSE TO CUSTOMERS

Steve Case appears to understand the need for the CEO to – in words he draws from his stint with Pizza Hut – sit taste bud to taste bud with your customer.[8] That means you don't settle solely for reports from underlings on your buyers, you maintain direct contact. Some of the ways Case makes it happen:

- "[H]e spends time lurking all over the America Online universe as if he were an average user, but under several secret screen names." – *The Washington Post*[9]
- "[He] also encouraged the tendency of his customers to say immediately and stridently what they thought of the service. Now a staff of two dozen people read his e-mail." – *The New York Times*[10]
- "The key to his success has been in understanding how an existing technology could affect ordinary people, making that idea accessible to a mass audience, and then marketing the heck out of it." – *US News & World Report*[11]
- "And AOL, in turn, was catering to its base, frequently splitting its shares to keep the price low." – *Money* magazine[12]

DISTINGUISH YOUR MEANS FROM CUSTOMER ENDS

Perhaps the greatest single insight that Steve Case gained from his focus on customers is that very few of them give a byte about the technology that enables their online adventures. And by that insight Case was able to differentiate AOL from all of its competitors – all of which apparently assume that consumers are as entranced by the technology as are the geeks who launched those firms.

> "We don't really care about the technology."
> – Steve Case

"We don't really care about the technology," Case told *Time* magazine in 1997. "We've tried to recognize that it is a means to an end, and the end is to improve the way people get information and communicate."[13]

That critical distinction between means and ends lifted Case's company to one of the highest valuations in the world, providing the monetary clout to buy one of the oldest and most powerful media conglomerates. *Newsweek* succinctly stated Case's key to success following the AOL–Time Warner merger announcement, noting that in paying attention to users, "Case discovered that his customers were most interested in chatting – usually about sex, it turns out – but in any case they cared more about easy access to each other than mastering the latest techie tricks."[14]

"Steve was the first person to understand that cyberspace could be a consumer product and like any brand, it needed to be sold," says an analyst who followed AOL from its inception. "That may seem obvious now, but that is what made his company special."[15]

A clue to Case's regard for the proper place of technology within AOL is perhaps contained in the company's mission statement, which says AOL will make the Internet as central to people's lives as the telephone and television, and even more valuable. How many families buy phones and TVs to gather 'round them at night and admire their technology? "Case and other AOL officials ... have always understood that technology is only the enabler of an online business, not the central attraction," commented *The Wall Street Journal*. "By contrast, Netscape was all about cutting-edge technology, and seemed to aim its products at people and businesses already a part of the techie club – the type that are connected to the Internet using the fastest computers and the highest-speed wires."[16] AOL bought Netscape in 1998.

AOL previously bought CompuServe, which, in *Time*'s words, was but one company which "bet that the real lure would be lots of fancy computer features. Case ... knew better ... AOL would reek with simplicity."[17]

SELL THE SIZZLE, NOT THE STEAK

Some people, but not many, ride roller coasters to admire the structural engineering and physics of the contraptions. Some people, but not many, visit Disney World to observe the animatronics that seems to give life to mechanical instruments. And some people, but not many, use computers to understand the capabilities of modern electronic technologies.

Steve Case understands why most people use computers: "Consumers don't care whether they're on a TCP/IP data network

HOW AOL SCORED BIG WITH CUSTOMERS[18]

Writing in a 1997 issue of *Forbes* magazine, commentator Guy Kawasaki offered these reasons that AOL would not meet the dire fate predicted for it by the company's detractors:

- First, you can access AOL almost anywhere with a local call. Getting AOL e-mail in Tokyo is no more difficult or expensive than getting it in New York.
- Second, AOL costs $20 a month for unlimited use. This is the 1990s equivalent of Federal Express' curve-jumping decision to charge one price for shipping a package no matter where it was going.
- Third, ... AOL passes the mother-in-law test ... For most people, the easiest way to use e-mail and browse the Internet is to join AOL.
- Fourth, AOL has achieved the status of a brand.
- Fifth, AOL has created a strong sense of community ... These relationships transcend the anonymity, aloofness and occasional cruelty of the Internet.

or an X.zS data network. They don't care if the content was created in HTML format or a Rainman format. They care about the experience."[19] Which is also what the vast majority of roller coaster riders and Disney World visitors care about.

Case's understanding that "the experience" – not the mechanics – is the object of computer use by most people, is the breakthrough realization that allowed him to take AOL where no company has gone before. AOL employees, Case says, "are really focused on providing a quality experience for millions of people."[20]

"The experience" is what makes AOL's prime objective strikingly similar to that of another spectacularly successful company, Walt Disney. As defenders of AOL wrote in *Upside* magazine, the folks who "wander down AOL's virtual Main Street USA" look for "the same sort of thing you'd expect to find in Disney World: recreation and entertainment, movie stars and TV personalities, and store fronts with cool stuff to buy."

The essential element that allows "the experience" is what Case and other AOL executives call context. As explained by the same *Upside* commentators, "AOL executives believe that if you get people together, entertain them with cool content, give them whatever information and services they need to make their lives easier and more convenient, and enable them to share their interests – *voilà*, you've got both 'community' and a collection of 'communities' coalescing around the dominant interest areas."[21]

"The experience" is what so many executives – absorbed, understandably enough, by the industries in which they work – overlook, because they're focused of necessity on mechanics. That's why AOL's "fast-growing popularity always remained inexplicable to the elite of the Internet," remarks *The Wall Street Journal*. "They missed the point, of course, that most average users wanted a convenient, low-tech way to be part of this great new communications medium."[22]

WHY A NO-COST WEB DIDN'T SINK AOL

As the World Wide Web became more accessible to more people in the mid-1990s, predictions of the impending demise of AOL – which was said by some observers to charge $20 a month for Web guide service – increased from their normal number to record levels. But AOL, far from losing its value, gained subscribers as never before. Here's why:

- "This year, America Online became a significant on-ramp to the Internet's vast network of highways, providing AOL subscribers with simple and affordable access to the Internet's most popular features. 'We believe most consumers will want to get Internet access the same way they access all of their other online services, so we intend to continue to extend the Internet offerings of the AOL brand to include all popular Internet features and capabilities, including World Wide Web ...' said Case. 'But in addition to providing full Internet access to AOL subscribers, we intend to aggressively develop completely new and independent Internet-centric businesses.'" – AOL corporate statement, September 7, 1994
- "Let's imagine AOL didn't exist today and the Net did. The Internet basically is this broken-up world. Consumers would hook up with service providers and buy this software package and that software package with plug-ins and add-ons to enable the experience. They would surf the Net and subscribe to services they want on an *à la carte* basis. Which is probably fine for a technologically astute early adopter but seems awfully complicated for a consumer market. TV would never have gotten a 90 percent market penetration if it had been that hard." – Steve Case in *Forbes*, October 7, 1996[23]

- "One measure of AOL's success in content is how subscribers use the system, which has become one of the most popular gateways to the World Wide Web. The company says users still spend 35 percent of their time in AOL's proprietary content areas." – *Business Week*, September 22, 1997[24]

- "And three or four years ago, when the Internet was coming into fruition, people were saying, 'Well, people don't really need this context thing. With all the stuff there, they'll just go directly to it.' And we said, 'Well, I guess that's possible.' But the more likely scenario, it seemed to us, was that consumers really would want some simplicity and sort of not have to find the needle in the haystack, and be able to find easily the stock quote they wanted or the sports quote they wanted, the weather they wanted or talk to people they are interested in, and so forth." – Steve Case at the National Press Club, October 26, 1998[25]

- "[AOL] transformed itself from a proprietary online service into an Internet service provider; then, when the riches of the Web appeared to render its exclusive content and cheesy graphics redundant, it showed that it understood the needs and tastes of ordinary consumers far better than its geeky critics." – *The Economist*, August 14, 1999[26]

- "AOL survived, and then flourished, by becoming a value-added Internet service provider, by giving content providers a better deal, by selling advertising, and by exploiting certain respects in which the Web's user interface remained behind AOL's." – Vermeer Technologies founder Charles H. Ferguson, in his book *High Stakes, No Prisoners*[27]

DELIVER HIGH VALUE AHEAD OF LOW PRICE

Price is about your money; value is about your money's worth. "Worth" is the only difference between the two, and it means everything. It's how Nordstrom's succeeds in a world of Sears, how Starbuck's becomes ubiquitous when there's Maxwell House; why FedEx isn't displaced by the Postal Service.

So how's this for value? AOL charges for services that are increasingly provided free to anyone willing to expend a little upfront energy to set them up. And AOL continues to swamp its low- and no-cost competitors. It draws head-shaking admiration from people such as the Silicon Valley analyst who says, "This company pioneered the model of content and access: You spend $22 [a month] to get specific information. A lot of companies would kill to have anyone pay for their service."[28]

> "If you want to reach a mainstream audience, you have to make it more plug and play. One-stop shopping. One disk to install. One price to pay."
> – Steve Case

Why do they pay for AOL? *Time* says it's those who "wanted the Net organized and edited for them ... Everything is as neatly organized as a small-town library ... Above all, need we mention, the goal is to make the Net seem well worth paying for."[29]

And that it is, for those whom *The New York Times* described as "the many adults who are unsure of their technological sea legs." They regard AOL as "the great life vest of cyberspace."[30]

AOL's value also lays in its efficiency, according to COO Bob Pittman: "You can pay your bills online instead of going to the post office … Time is a precious commodity, and AOL will save you time."[31]

And will provide convenience: "If you want to reach a mainstream audience, you have to make it more plug and play," Steve Case says. "One-stop shopping. One disk to install. One price to pay. One customer service number to call."[32] It amounts to what Case calls "a sense of order in kind of a sea of chaos. And that's really been a core differentiator for AOL."[33]

IGNORE "IRRELEVANT" EXPERTS – CUSTOMERS RULE!

Steve Case has never hidden the key reason for AOL's success: He says the company simply listens to customers. That's apparently not so simple for the many firms – most AOL competitors among them – that fail to do it. But you can bring AOL-like customer focus to your company if you:

• *Let no one but customers shape your business.* Steve Case is willing to roll with the punches from every sort of so-called expert, so long as he stays focused on consumers and provides what they want. When you're customer-centric in deed as well as words, the only hurt you'll suffer from punches thrown by others will result from laughing at them.

• *Distinguish your means from customer ends.* While techno-wizards were consumed with the techno-wizardry of their products and services, Case was consumed with providing the simplicity and sense of community that consumers said they really wanted from an online service. Understand the difference between the results customers want from your offerings and the means by which you'll deliver what they want. That's how AOL soared.

- *Sell the sizzle, not the steak.* "Experience" is a word used often by AOL leaders – applying it not to their background or past jobs, but to the customer's interaction with AOL. Case and his team know that the most critical aspect of users' time online is not what they're doing, but how they *feel* about what they're doing. It's a distinction with a huge difference for any product or service.

- *Deliver high value ahead of low price.* If value didn't matter, the word "premium" would be a death knell in commerce. People by the millions pay AOL for what they could get elsewhere at little or no cost (in money) because the service is well worth it. Giving folks what they regard as their money's worth can raise your company's worth sky high.

NOTES

1. Rajiv Chandrasekaran, "A Case of Timing, Knowledge," *The Washington Post,* January 11, 2000.

2. Uncredited, "Pricks and Kicks," *The Economist* (US edition), August 14, 1999.

3. Saul Hansell, "America Online's Triumvirate in Cyberspace," *The New York Times,* February 16, 1998. .

4. Walter S. Mossberg, "If the Techies Hate the AOL–Netscape Deal, It Must Be Good for Us," *The Wall Street Journal*, December 3, 1998.

5. Gene Koprowski, "AOL CEO Steve Case," *Forbes ASAP*, October 7, 1996.

6. Curt Monash and Linda Barlow, "AOL Doesn't Suck!" *Upside*, May 1997.

7. Amy Cortese and Amy Barrett, "The Online World of Steve Case," *Business Week*, April 15, 1996.

8. Joshua Cooper Ramo, "How AOL Lost the Battles but Won the War," *Time*, September 22, 1997.

9. Kara Swisher, "Steve Case Tries to Hold a Place Online," *The Washington Post*, August 27, 1995.

10. Saul Hansell, "America Online's Triumvirate in Cyberspace," *The New York Times*, February 16, 1998.

11. Fred Vogelstein, "The Talented Mr. Case," *US News & World Report*, January 24, 2000.

12. John Helyar, "If You Want to Understand What's Happened to the Stock Market in the Past Three Years Just Look at America Online," *Money*, October 1999.

13. Joshua Cooper Ramo, "How AOL Lost the Battles but Won the War," *Time*, September 22, 1997.

14. Jared Sandberg, "Case Study," *Newsweek*, January 24, 2000.

15. Kara Swisher, "Steve Case Tries to Hold a Place Online," *The Washington Post*, August 27, 1995.

16. Walter S. Mossberg, "If the Techies Hate the AOL–Netscape Deal, It Must Be Good for Us," *The Wall Street Journal*, December 3, 1998.

17. Joshua Cooper Ramo, "How AOL Lost the Battles but Won the War," *Time*, September 22, 1997.

18. Guy Kawasaki, "Get Off Steve's Case," *Forbes*, January 27, 1997.

19. Gene Koprowski, "AOL CEO Steve Case," *Forbes ASAP*, October 7, 1996.

20. National Public Radio, "All Things Considered," December 5, 1996.

21. Curt Monash and Linda Barlow, "AOL Doesn't Suck!" *Upside*, May 1997.

22. Kara Swisher, "How Steve Case Morphed Into a Media Mogul," *The Wall Street Journal*, January 11, 2000.

23. Gene Koprowski, "AOL CEO Steve Case," *Forbes ASAP*, October 7, 1996.

24. Catherine Yang, "Answered Prayers at America Online," *Business Week*, September 22, 1997.

25. Speech at National Press Club, Federal News Service transcript, October 26, 1998.

26. Uncredited, "Pricks and Kicks," *The Economist* (US edition), August 14, 1999.

27. Charles H. Ferguson, *High Stakes, No Prisoners*, Times Business, New York, 1999.

28. Jon Swartz, "Case Study – A Look at Mr. America Online," *The San Francisco Chronicle*, February 22, 1999.

29. Joshua Cooper Ramo, "How AOL Lost the Battles but Won the War," *Time*, September 22, 1997.

30. Saul Hansell, "Now, AOL Everywhere," *The New York Times*, July 4, 1999.

31. Curt Monash and Linda Barlow, "AOL Doesn't Suck!" *Upside*, May 1997.

32. Gene Koprowski, "AOL CEO Steve Case," *Forbes ASAP*, October 7, 1996.

33. Speech at National Press Club, Federal News Service transcript, October 26, 1998.

Six

DON'T SHY FROM A FIGHT ...

IN THIS CHAPTER

Competing successfully in the digital age means playing by new rules – and many of the old ones. Among the latter: You've still got to stay close to customers and respond to their changing needs. Among the new rules: Your company is as likely to be toppled by a presumed pipsqueak as by a market leader. AOL is the biggest winner among Internet companies thus far because it, unlike most other firms that have tried to capitalize on the information revolution, has recognized (or divined) what's new and what's not in the competitive arena. Here are the keys to AOL's triumphs over all rivals.

In the space of about seven years, AOL went from also-ran in a line of business (proprietary online service) presumed to be terminal to undisputed industry leader targeted for attack by companies ranging from global conglomerates to kitchen-table entrepreneurs. "There are a bunch of people who believe it's their manifest destiny to put AOL out of business," says Steve Case, who was only recently among the outsiders who assaulted entrenched corporate giants. "And it's my job to make sure that doesn't happen."[1]

If he retains his feel for the right moves in battling foes, he'll do the job well.

OBSERVE THE NEW RULES OF CORPORATE COMBAT

"Sometime in 1994, AOL got it, the only established company that did." Those are words of Vermeer Technologies founder

Charles H. Ferguson, writing in his book *High Stakes, No Prisoners*.[2] What AOL got, Ferguson asserts, is "the importance of
the Internet." AOL also "differentiated itself from Prodigy and
CompuServe (which at the time were the far larger incumbents)
by adopting more modern technology," such as the Windows
graphical user interface and minicomputers rather than main-
frames to deliver its service.

> "Sometime in 1994, AOL got it, the only established company that did." – Charles H. Ferguson

But AOL also "got" something that's probably been more
consequential to its subsequent success: the
new shape of business in the Internet
age. That was hinted at in a 1993
comment by a technology industry
researcher who termed AOL "hipper, cooler, and faster on its feet"
than its rivals. That was certainly true
in comparing AOL with its then-big-
gest rival, Prodigy, which *The Washington
Post* termed "slow to adapt to the marketplace …
like its giant owners": IBM and Sears.[3]

It can be argued that AOL's rise within a new competitive landscape resulted in large measure from its display of what business
professors David Yoffie and Michael Cusumano call "the three
main principles of judo strategy: rapid movement, flexibility,
and leverage." Explaining judo strategy in a 1999 article in the
Harvard Business Review, Yoffie and Cusumano expand on the
three principles and their execution:

1. *Move rapidly to uncontested ground to avoid head-to-head con-
    flict.* Move to new products, move to new pricing models,
    move to new testing and distribution models – all to keep
    out of the way of bigger, stronger competitors or to move
    where those competitors (usually owing to size) can't go.

2. *Be flexible and give way when attacked directly by superior force.* Mesh flexibility and tactical adjustments with ongoing strategic plans.

3. *Exploit leverage that uses the weight and strength of opponents against them.* A competitor's weight and strength, for example, in the form of strategic commitments and investments, can be confining in the face of nimbleness.[4]

The means by which AOL rose to preeminence in the 1990s exemplifies these principles. To vault past Prodigy and CompuServe, AOL delivered a product that most new users regarded as more valuable, and it dared to introduce a flat-rate pricing model. As for flexibility, AOL's is regarded by some as extreme, but by all as effective (*see "Reshape Everything but Your Vision" Chapter 1, p.30*). And AOL is among the most effective firms in forming alliances with best competitors of all sizes (*see next chapter*).

FOCUS MORE ON CUSTOMERS THAN COMPETITORS

In advocating "judo strategy" for success in today's competitive environment, professors Yoffie and Cusumano advise firms to "mesh flexibility and tactical adjustments with long-term strategic plans." AOL has masterfully balanced short-term flexibility with long-term consistency: Steve Case's vision and AOL's mission have continuously aimed at wiring individuals to the outside world and to each other, while tactics required to make that happen seem to have been regarded as changeable as the weather.

With this unbroken focus on its ultimate aim, AOL has managed to avoid being lured by competition alone into markets or lines of business that don't fit with its mission. Its battle, in the words of *The New York Times*, is to become the "operating system ... for daily life," which involves providing the means for people to "wire their families, their finances, their jobs – even their household appliances – into one vast network."[5]

AOL may bring to bear a vast range of products and services – so broad as to require the company's linking with the Time Warner empire, plus other acquisitions and strategic partners – in pursuit of its overriding objective. But there's been no confusion, even from the days before AOL was known by its current name, about what the company wanted to be when it grew up. At a minimum, Steve Case speaks for himself and AOL's top echelon when he says, "I think we are every day waking up saying: How can we build a better service for our members? How can we build a better company to work for, to invest in? And how can we participate in building a medium that we can be proud of?"

That the answers to these questions include fierce competition is something that comes with the territory, Case implies: "That's what makes it challenging; it's also what makes it fun. We have thousands of competitors ... all trying to do a better job of meeting the needs of this growing audience. And that's really what makes this so exciting ... We're trying to do the better job than anybody else in creating a great service, a great company, and a great medium."[6]

Microsoft, in apparent contrast to AOL, seems less to pursue a long-term vision of whom it wishes to serve than to pursue a changing line-up of targeted competitors. As *The Economist* notes, Microsoft "is never happier than when chasing a company it has decided is its enemy."[7]

Microsoft's long-term direction – at least at the time this volume is being written – appears insufficiently clear to even determine the enemy that tops the company's most-wanted list. *The New York Times* recounts a June 1999 internal meeting at Microsoft that established "the company's new strategy for MSN – the latest of several over the last five years, as Microsoft has struggled, uncharacteristically, to find its place on the Web."[8]

By some accounts, AOL is MS Enemy #1. But some observers question that, as did *The Wall Street Journal* just after the AOL–Time Warner merger was announced: "Having dabbled in media, Microsoft has reverted to being primarily a software-technology company."[9] *Newsweek* found a similar divergence, noting that, "While both Microsoft and AOL share a vision that the Net will be everywhere, Gates and Ballmer think the key to unlocking value isn't owning a movie studio, but producing the software that will make the whole caboodle click."[10] Bill Gates's relinquishing his chairman title to ostensibly become chief software architect conforms to Microsoft's supposed new strategic direction.

> "I think we are every day waking up saying: How can we build a better service for our members?"
> – Steve Case

Ironically, Microsoft's seeming inconstancy in knowing where it wants to go over the long haul may constrain where it is able to go without tripping over its own feet. As *Business Week* puts it, "Microsoft is wrestling with conflicting goals. It wants to maintain the PC's dominance while it goes after info appliances. 'Microsoft doesn't want to cannibalize the market,' says Rob Enderle, vice president at Giga Information Group. 'If Web appliances are too good a solution, they lose revenue.' "[11]

In the same article, Steve Case displays his continuing adherence to a single, overarching vision in dismissing the suggestion that AOL is expanding in such a way as to go head-to-head with Microsoft in the software arena: "We have no interest in being in the operating systems business – not now, not ever."[12]

AOL'S COMPETITORS, PART I: THAT WAS THEN ...

In the mid-1990s, AOL's online proprietary service soared from a distant third place in subscribers, behind CompuServe and Prodigy, to leave both in the dust – at the same time leaving Microsoft's 1994 launch of the rival MSN a virtual nonstarter. How did they do that? (Italics added for emphasis.)

- *"Case ... spent heavily on marketing.* It was an aggressive move to get a jump on rivals Prodigy and CompuServe. Many worried that AOL was spending too much selling the product and not enough on the product itself ... In 1993, AOL introduced a Windows-based version of its online software, luring more subscribers. In the next twelve months, AOL membership tripled to one million ... Around that time Microsoft waded into the market with Microsoft Network. AOL countered by bulking up its service with more multimedia shopping, more content, and more links to the Internet." – *The Washington Times*, January 11, 2000[13]
- *"AOL really went into hyperdrive* ... by simplifying its pricing structure and drastically lowering hourly rates to $9.95 for five hours a month. By comparison, the pricing of CompuServe and Prodigy is more cumbersome, featuring various plans and optional services that carry extra charges. Consumers obviously voted for simple,

and AOL began to attract subscribers and content vendors, who knew a good thing when they saw it." – *The San Francisco Chronicle*, August 3, 1994[14]

- *"Aggressive marketing and lots of content* made AOL the No. 1 online player. The plan: Keep boosting market share, both on its own and through its deals with other distributors like AT&T ... [T]he bet is that most consumers will want to stick with AOL's brand-name content rather than roam the Web." – *Business Week*, April 15, 1996[15]

- *"AOL has become the cyberspace town square.* It's the place to go to mouth off about the O.J. Simpson trials or your annoying boyfriend." – *MediaWeek*, December 2, 1996[16]

- *"It all worked.* AOL went public ... with fewer than 200,000 subscribers. Today that number is 14 million and climbing, courtesy of a laser-beam consumer focus ... [T]hrough hundreds of sales alliances with companies, from Barnes & Noble to 1-800-FLOWERS, that audience is getting accustomed to the idea of the Net as one vast cash register." – *Time*, December 7, 1998[17]

MAKE THE MOST OF BEING SMALL

Throughout its history, AOL has used its size – both when it was the smallest of proprietary online service providers and today, when it's the Net's Goliath – to great advantage. Back at the dawn of the wired world's evolutionary history (in the early 1990s), when AOL was equivalent to the tiny mammalian tree shrew that flitted among seemingly invincible dinosaurs, the company at first survived and later began to grow by capitalizing on advantages of being small, such as:

- *Playing the underdog.* Most people who otherwise lack any persuasive reason to favor one combatant over another will by emotion affix themselves to the guy who's given little chance of success. Thus, for example, public sentiment in the US was strongly with AOL when Microsoft said it would bundle its MSN service with its near-universal Windows operating system.

• *Maneuvering beneath larger rivals' radar.* Prodigy was a joint venture of IBM and Sears. CompuServe was owned by H&R Block. MSN was created by Microsoft. And through the years when it faced and defeated each of these services, AOL had no corporate parent or significant backing. Why wouldn't it be virtually ignored at first by the others? Why wouldn't Bill Gates tell Steve Case, "I can go into this business myself and bury you"?

• *Capitalizing on a lean structure.* A young, small company may lack financial wherewithal, but it also may operate without an entrenched bureaucracy or decisions based on "that's the way we do it here." It's at least highly questionable that AOL would have in effect bet its existence on the famously successful free-trial, "carpet-bombing" marketing campaign had the decision to do so involved many more officials than CEO Case and marketing chief Jan Brandt.

• *Gaining the adrenalin boost of fighting for survival.* There may be nothing in business so motivating as the prospect of being obliterated if you don't perform. Steve Case – in giving up a secure, if unexciting, marketing position with firmly entrenched Pepsico to join a shaky company in an infant industry – bet his career that he was not hallucinating in envisioning a wired world. It was more than enough of a gamble to spur remarkable achievement.

AOL'S COMPETITORS, PART II:
... AND THIS IS NOW

A fearsome collection of long-established companies such as AT&T and superstar start-ups led by Yahoo were gunning for AOL before the Time Warner deal was announced. Now, there are few firms in any aspect of media, communications, or the Internet that don't want at least a piece of the empire that AOL will control. Here are representative comments on the anticipated battlefields and combatants. (Italics added for emphasis.)

- *"Where is the value, the potential profit, in the emerging business model for the New Economy? Is it GM's OnStar technology? Or the net-*work service provided by AOL? Or the online content, which is after all why AOL wants to merge with Time Warner? Who is going to control the value of the new in-car Internet services? Who will control it in the network in the intelligent kitchen where your fridge or kitchen bin can re-order from the supermarket, and a food company such as Kraft can download recipes and order ingredients for you? ... [T]he answer is none of the above. The value lies entirely in the possibility of these alliances; it is in the network, not in any one of its components ... [T]he key is 'D2D,' or device to device. It is ... the possibility that your kitchen gadgets will be able to make their own phone calls and speak to the supermarket's computer."* – *The Independent* [London], February 22, 2000[18]
- *"During the strategic review that led to the Time Warner deal,* Case and his senior staff surveyed a broad landscape and raised the names of such targets as eBay, Amazon.com, Intuit, and Bell Atlantic. The ink on the agreement was still wet when Merrill Lynch's Internet guru, Henry Blodget, speculated that America Online might go after Wal-Mart next. Not likely, Case says. But, he says, America

Online does want to become a Wal-Mart-style superstore of interactivity, linking people to each other and to information, entertainment, shopping, and learning through a variety of devices, including PC, TV, and phone." – *Fortune*, February 7, 2000[19]

- *"Now Case is gambling* that as e-commerce grows from a novelty to the bedrock of 21st century capitalism, AOL can – perhaps must – become a major player in the lucrative 'enterprise' market, helping corporations large and small move their operations online … It's another smart plan, but executing this one will mean battling not upstarts like Prodigy and CompuServe but behemoths like IBM and Microsoft." – *Time*, December 7, 1998[20]

- *"Microsoft is setting out to improve its Web technology,* market aggressively, cut distribution deals with industry partners – and, ultimately, change the economics of the online business … [E]xecutives here are encouraged by signs of improvement in the last few months – rising traffic at MSN, favorable trade-press reviews for recently improved features, and, last December, the second-highest monthly increase in five years in new subscribers to the MSN Internet access service." – *The New York Times*, February 13, 2000[21]

- *"Yahoo's Web site has resembled an incredibly busy airport hub.* Everyone passes through it, even if they really want to head somewhere else … Yahoo has also become one of the few new Internet companies to report consistent profits before acquisition charges. That has made it a darling among stock-market investors … So far, Yahoo has chosen to line up most of its content from dozens of independent sources. That has kept costs down and has given Yahoo maximum flexibility to add whatever services users want. But it means Yahoo doesn't have anything quite like the high-powered marketing pipeline that AOL and Time Warner could create for movies, music, and magazines …" – *The Wall Street Journal*, January 11, 2000[22]

MAKE THE MOST OF BEING BIG

Today AOL, in sharp contrast to its scrawny stature of less than 10 years ago, stands as what *Fortune* calls a "customer-focused behemoth – if that's not a contradiction in terms – that will be a force in media, communications, retailing, financial services, health care, education, and travel ..."[23] Capitalizing on smallness is hardly an option. But the company shows signs that it can be equally inventive and adept at throwing its weight around, for example, by:

- *Using core strength to build other strengths.* "[T]hink of AOL's core online service as the locomotive that drives a bigger, more complex enterprise," suggests *Fortune*, "that can be deployed to smash barriers to entry and clear the way for building new businesses. Even before the Time Warner deal, America Online had grown from a company that focused on one brand (AOL) for one platform (the PC) in one country (the US) to a company with many brands (CompuServe, Netscape, ICQ, Digital City, MovieFone, Spinner, iPlanet, and MapQuest) for many platforms (TVs, phones, etc.) that are distributed in seven languages and 15 countries."[24]

- *Preparing for the demise of your cash cow.* More than half of AOL's revenue is derived from the monthly fees from 22 million subscribers to its dial-up Internet access business. Correctly recognizing that competitors will eventually either get a significant piece of that business – thus far a failed effort by MSN – or destroy it – a potentially successful attack by the likes of NetZero and Juno – AOL has for some time been building new revenue sources, primarily from advertising and new services.

- *Guarding against becoming a victim of its own successful strategy.* Case is well aware that another would-be giant killer could follow his lead: emerge from obscurity and topple the market leader – now AOL. When he met Sky Dayton (then 26), founder of the successful, although still comparatively small, Internet service provider called EarthLink, Case said, "I'm not going to let you sneak up on me like we snuck up on CompuServe and Prodigy."[25]

"I'm not going to let you sneak up on me like we snuck up on CompuServe and Prodigy."
– Steve Case to EarthLink founder Sky Dayton

- *Retaining entrepreneurial energy.* Although it pursues acquisitions and alliances on their own merits, the now-big AOL also actively seeks infusions of think-small corporate cultures in its deals with other firms. "Indeed, its $4.2 billion acquisition of Netscape Communications," according to *The New York Times*, "was meant to inject Silicon Valley culture into AOL and to create a home base from which to acquire more West Coast start-ups ..."[26]

- *Disclaiming the power of predominance.* AOL wishes to gain as many customers as it can get – without incurring charges of exercising monopoly power from government watchdogs. So Case contends, for example, "We don't have anything remotely monopolistic. We have a little over half of the online audience, and there are plenty of competitors – ranging from 5,000 [Internet service providers] and startups to big-momma companies like Microsoft, AT&T, and Disney."[27]

DON'T SHY FROM A FIGHT ...

Business battles for the minds and money of customers have never been hotter or faster than they are today among the countless companies seeking to cash in on burgeoning Internet-based commerce. And no combatant has been as lightly regarded and spectacularly successful as AOL. The company's ascent results from adhering to key guidelines that can also boost your enterprise to unprecedented achievements:

- *Observe the new rules of corporate combat.* The rapid-fire introduction and development of new information technologies has brought dramatic changes to commercial competition – favoring the companies that best discern the nature, shape, and implications of those changes. AOL's experience demonstrates the rewards that can be realized by being out front in anticipating and capitalizing on the new, new things.

- *Focus more on customers than competitors.* AOL seems not to compete as much for the sake of competition itself as it does because taking on rivals is a necessary part of pursuing its mission. The distinction may be subtle, but also telling: the company whose aim is to go after other firms, rather than customers, can go off on a tangent.

- *Make the most of being small.* In business today, perhaps more than ever before, small is beautiful – but only if you make it so by exploiting emerging advantages that can accrue to the small at the expense of the large. AOL showed how it can be done – leaving defeated giants to dust themselves off and figure out what hit them.

- *Make the most of being big.* Size no longer confers upon its possessors the advantages enjoyed by many companies through most of the 20th century – as firms such as IBM and AT&T learned. But the astute enterprise that identifies the new and changed ways in which big can still be best, as AOL appears thus far to have done, will give itself every opportunity to keep on growing.

NOTES

1. Marc Gunther, "The Internet Is Mr. Case's Neighborhood," *Fortune*, March 30, 1998.

2. Charles H. Ferguson, *High Stakes, No Prisoners*, Times Business, New York, 1999.

3. Daniel Southerland, "America Online's Rapid Rise," *The Washington Post*, November 8, 1993.

4. David Yoffie and Michael Cusumano, "Judo Strategy: The Competitive Dynamics of Internet Time," *Harvard Business Review*, January/February 1999.

5. Saul Hansell, "Now, AOL Everywhere," *The New York Times*, July 4, 1999.

6. Speech at National Press Club, Federal News Service transcript, October 26, 1998.

7. Uncredited, "Pricks and Kicks," *The Economist* (US edition), August 14, 1999.

8. Steve Lohr, "Again, It's Microsoft vs. the World," *The New York Times*, February 13, 2000.

9. Uncredited, "How AOL–Time Warner Deal May Affect Other Players," *The Wall Street Journal*, January 11, 2000.

10. Steven Levy, "The Two Big Bets," *Newsweek*, January 24, 2000.

11. Catherine Yang, "There's No Escaping AOL," *Business Week*, December 6, 1999.

12. Catherine Yang, "There's No Escaping AOL," *Business Week*, December 6, 1999.

13. Timothy Burn, "Case Gets Last Laugh: AOL Grew From Humble Beginnings," *The Washington Times*, January 11, 2000.

14. David Einstein, "America Online Hits the Fast Track," *The San Francisco Chronicle*, August 3, 1994.

15. Amy Cortese and Amy Barrett, "The Online World of Steve Case," *Business Week*, April 15, 1996.

16. Cathy Taylor, "Welcome! You've Got Bob Pittman," *MediaWeek*, December 2, 1996.

17. Michael Krantz, "AOL, You've Got Netscape," *Time*, December 7, 1998.

18. Diane Coyle, "Firms Must Cast the Net Wide to Catch the New Economy's Customers," *The Independent* [London], February 22, 2000.

19. Marc Gunther, "These Guys Want It All," *Fortune*, February 7, 2000.

20. Michael Krantz, "AOL, You've Got Netscape," *Time*, December 7, 1998.

21. Steve Lohr, "Again, It's Microsoft vs. the World," *The New York Times*, February 13, 2000.

22. Uncredited, "How AOL–Time Warner Deal May Affect Other Players," *The Wall Street Journal*, January 11, 2000.

23. Marc Gunther, "These Guys Want It All," *Fortune*, February 7, 2000.

24. Marc Gunther, "These Guys Want It All," *Fortune*, February 7, 2000.

25. Marc Gunther, "The Internet Is Mr. Case's Neighborhood," *Fortune*, March 30, 1998.

26. Saul Hansell, "Now, AOL Everywhere," *The New York Times*, July 4, 1999.

27. Jon Swartz, "Case Study – A Look at Mr. America Online," *The San Francisco Chronicle*, February 22, 1999.

Seven

... OR HESITATE TO SLEEP WITH THE ENEMY

IN THIS CHAPTER

In this information age, there's too much information; in our knowledge economy, there's too much knowledge. That is, there's too much information and knowledge for any one organization to develop and maintain the resources required to handle it all. So partnering and acquiring have gone beyond being strategic options; for an increasing number of firms, links with other companies are essential. And you probably can't do better than AOL if you seek a model for learning how to make alliances and acquisitions work. In 1999 alone, the company acquired seven other firms, made investments in 34 more, and struck or extended alliances with still others.[1] According to *TheStreet.com*, "experience suggests that if AOL is anything, it's a dealmaking shop."[2] Here's how that shop makes deals.

Steve Case appears to recognize no barriers to potential cooperation or buy-out talks with other companies – least of all that another firm is considered the closest thing you have to a mortal enemy. When AOL and Time Warner announced their plan to merge, for example, most observers assumed the deal would spell the end of AOL's joint ventures with German media giant and Time Warner arch-foe Bertelsmann. Case thinks otherwise, saying AOL and Bertelsmann are talking about "how to work together in the future." The CEO adds, "We're confident we'll have a good relationship with them."[3]

It's hardly the first time Case sees opportunity where others see impossibility. He'd previously shocked the business world with deals such as acquisition of supposed enemy CompuServe and alliance in several areas with Microsoft. It's increasingly clear that Case's deals reflect a new and rapidly emerging consensus that companies often have more to gain from love – or at least peaceful coexistence – than war.

PUT COKE VS. PEPSI IN A MUSEUM

In the relatively well ordered, predictable business universe that prevailed through most of the 20th century, we were safe in assuming the constancy of certain mutual hatreds: Ford vs. General Motors, for example, Avis vs. Hertz, Coke vs. Pepsi, and Wile E. Coyote vs. the Road Runner.

"My only competition is with myself."
– Venture fund general partner Charles Lax

But today, although those rivalries may endure, a great many others are subject to dramatic reversal at almost any time. "My only competition is with myself," says venture fund general partner Charles Lax, who told *The Wall Street Journal* that he doesn't hesitate to do business with the "enemy," adding, "We co-invest with AOL and CMGI," companies whose Web portals (CMGI's is AltaVista) are archrivals of Yahoo, in which Lax's fund holds a substantial stake.[4]

"Cross-investing is only one of the ways some once-sworn foes are cooperating," the *Journal* notes. "The convergence of the Internet, media, and entertainment companies has created some strange bedfellows, with the proposed mega-merger of America Online and Time Warner Inc. ... just adding to the overlap."

The trend caught the *Journal*'s attention some time ago; for example, soon after AOL signed a 1996 deal with AT&T, which at the time was considered by many observers to be the chief threat to AOL's long-term health and welfare. "It's driving me nuts. My head hurts right now," the head of a communications research firm complained. "Everybody wants to find his place at the orgy, and if you don't get your mattress staked out now, you may miss it completely."[5]

What gives? Sleeping with the enemy is a means of hedging one's bets, said then-chairman of then-independent Netscape, Jim Clark, speaking of AOL 's shocking agreement with supposedly despised Microsoft to offer its subscribers the Internet Explorer Web browser. Clark found Case to be "like a chameleon – like any good businessman who will change to suit the needs of the market."[6]

Four years later, following the AOL–Time Warner deal, the *Journal* sought an opinion on declining enmity in enterprise from business professor Barry J. Nalebuff. "We're at a stage where there's a transformation of the economic infrastructure. It's too big a problem for any one company to solve. So you cooperate," said the co-author of a book entitled *Co-opetition*. Echoing Clark's notion of hedging bets, Nalebuff adds, "you don't try to be too smart. If you own a piece of all the players, then if the pie grows, no matter who succeeds you succeed."

Under what circumstances is partnering supplanted by purchasing? "That's a complicated question," the *Journal* contends, looking at AOL for indications of the company's distinguishing criteria – and apparently finding nothing definitive. Within weeks of announcing the AOL–Time Warner deal, Case continued to make news with both pending and signed new partnerships involving so-called "old economy" retailer Sears,

THE BUYS THAT MADE TODAY'S AOL[8]

Among the more notable AOL acquisitions are these:

- *Redgate Communications*, in 1994, for $34 million – which made multimedia CD-ROMs and was headed by Ted Leonsis, still a top AOL executive;
- *ANS*, in 1994, for $35 million – a creator of the Internet that provided AOL with high-speed network capacity;
- *Medior*, in 1995, for $30 million – an interactive media developer founded by Barry Schuler, who has steadily risen in prominence at AOL;
- *Global Network Navigator*, in 1995, for $11 million – which provided the foundation for AOL's Net-based service, and was closed after AOL went to flat-rate pricing;
- *CompuServe*, in 1998 – in a multi-party deal under which WorldCom first bought all of the one-time online service provider. Then AOL gave WorldCom its ANS Communications network services division in exchange for CompuServe's subscriber base and online content operation plus $175 million;
- *Mirabilis*, in 1998, for $287 million – an Israeli company that came up with the ICQ (as in "I seek you") Web site and instant-messaging software;
- *Netscape Communications*, in 1999, for $4.2 billion – gave AOL the once high-flying Silicon Valley powerhouse that had previously turned down Steve Case's overtures for cooperation;
- *When.com*, in 1999, for an undisclosed amount – a provider of a personalized Internet calendar service and events listing;
- *MovieFone, Inc.*, in 1999, for $388 million – a movie listing guide and ticketing service; and
- *Spinner Networks, Inc.*, and *Nullsoft, Inc.*, in 1999, for $400 million – both providers of music via the Internet.

Roebuck and – yet again – presumed nemesis AT&T.[7]

ALLY AND BUY TO BE
EVERYTHING YOU AREN'T

Management experts generally agree that most companies are best advised to focus on what they do best. Stick with your core competencies, they say, don't be distracted by wandering into areas where you can't capitalize on your strengths.

So what's a company to do when it needs a non-core competency to support a core competency? AOL in its early years, for example, possessed the technical competency to deliver online information, but had no competency to speak of in developing online content.

> "Yet, with an impressive hat trick of three new partnerships last week, AOL has suddenly grabbed central stage in cyberspace."
> – The Wall Street Journal

The company found an answer in alliances. An early one with *The Chicago Tribune* is cited retrospectively as important to both AOL itself and the way online services subsequently developed. In 1991, AOL and the *Tribune* (which then owned 11 percent of AOL), "set up Chicago Online, an affiliated service that offers up-to-date information about Chicago produced by the *Tribune*," reported *The Washington Post*. "The newspaper, in turn, helps market America Online in the Chicago area."[9]

It wasn't long before *Business Week* would observe, "Deals are now key to America Online's growth. One of its best has been with SeniorNet, a group that encourages older consumers to use computers. SeniorNet promotes America Online to its 5,000 members, collecting a sales commission for each member who signs up. In return, America Online has added special services for older subscribers, including bulletin boards with news and information on special topics, such as health care and sex over 50."[10]

With these and other early links, according to a 1993 report in the magazine *Microtimes*, AOL differentiated itself from its competitors not only with its vaunted ease of use, but also with "its openness to outside partnerships and some aggressive marketing." By "[m]aking alliances the key to its growth," *The Washington Post* reported, "AOL turned its first profit within two years of its founding."[11]

And the company has only gotten more from its partnerships since. In 1996, for example, *The Wall Street Journal* observed, "A month ago, the nation's No. 1 online service faced the potent threat that the Internet might all but overwhelm it. Yet, with an impressive hat trick of three new partnerships last week, AOL has suddenly grabbed central stage in cyberspace."[12] *US News & World Report* was no less effusive at about the same time, saying that with its "headline-grabbing alliances," AOL "significantly expanded its distribution channels to gain additional users. As a result, AOL repositioned itself as a dominant presence on the Net – and in the online service business."[13]

Two years later, AOL used a simultaneous acquisition and alliance to address its relative lack of core competence in technology (a price of striving above all for simplicity). "How can the company possibly hope to compete in the corporate networking market if its own network is held together with

Scotch tape and baling wire?" *Time* asked rhetorically. "By marrying Netscape and taking Sun [Microsystems] as a mistress, that's how. Netscape gives Case both a battalion of geek programmers and the software they've been working on ... But the soul of AOL's newly empowered machine may turn out to be Scott McNealy, the brilliant, voluble CEO of Sun Microsystems," whose Java programming language and the products it enables "could finally break Microsoft's stranglehold on the digital universe."[14]

Fast-forward once more – to the year 2000 – and AOL is still making deals that latch onto world-class capabilities it won't have even after swallowing the Time Warner empire. Prime example, a pact with "old-economy" retailer Sears, Roebuck & Co. "that will put AOL in hundreds of stores and Sears on millions of computer screens," according to *The Los Angeles Times*. "Sears and AOL also will co-develop programming and products, taking the partnership beyond other 'click-and-mortar' alliances."[15]

AOL has been going beyond ordinary in tapping into other firms' strengths since it was a barely flickering light in the online universe. Its success in gaining best-available capabilities is instructive for any firm that wants to give and get competencies through others.

DISCOVER NEW WORLDS WITH PARTNERS AND PURCHASES

Gaining other firms' strengths that complement yours is an important reason for pursuing alliances and acquisitions. But such arrangements can also provide the wherewithal – other-

TWO DEALS THAT SHOOK
– AND SHAPED –
THE INTERNET

On November 24, 1998, AOL announced an acquisition and an alliance that rocked even the normally raucous and volatile world of Internet commerce. The company:

- bought Netscape Communications for $4.2 billion, grabbing the breakthrough Navigator browser, the Netcenter Website and its 9 million registered users, and the corporate e-commerce software that helped generate some 75 percent of Netscape's revenue; and
- partnered with Sun Microsystems in a comprehensive deal aimed at accelerating the partners' involvement in e-commerce and using Sun's Java technology to develop Internet devices that help Internet users access AOL brands.

According to *The Washington Post*, Steve Case, in making the deals:

"... succeeded where many have failed, in marrying, at least for the moment, industry titans that have played radically different roles in shaping the Internet. 'This will be biggest single development in the maturation of e-commerce,' [UUNet CEO John W.] Sidgmore said of the deal. The Internet, he said, was developed by many small companies, all focused on their own distinctive bits and bytes. 'For the first time ever, you'll have a diverse family of products and technologies under the same umbrella.' "[16]

> The combinations were almost universally judged by outside observ-
> ers as striking at Microsoft and perhaps even leading to the day (still
> pending at the time this is written) that Windows would be unseated
> as virtually the sole way that consumers would access cyberspace.
> "There's at least an argument to be made that indeed there's some-
> body else on the block now," said UCLA business professor George
> Geis, "that AOL, Netscape, and Sun are quite formidable."[17]

wise lacking or perhaps too risky – to step into entirely new
business realms. That's what AOL has been doing, particularly
in its more recent history, by joining with other companies to
develop and provide futuristic products and services that were
once mentioned only within the confines of a world's fair or
Walt Disney's "Tomorrowland."

For example, in its series of partnerships forged to deliver "AOL
Anywhere" – that is, to make Web-access devices for every room
of the house and every phase of life – AOL is inking pacts with
companies such as Gateway Computer, with which AOL is developing and co-marketing devices such as Internet appliances
and Web terminals. Another deal puts AOL subscribers' e-mail
on Palm handheld devices that connect with the Web. An agreement with Motorola makes AOL Instant Messenger (AIM)
service available on Motorola's smart wireless devices. And in a
race with Microsoft to make the television an appliance that
accesses the Web as easily as network and cable broadcasts, AOL
is working with Hughes Electronics, Hughes Network Systems,
Philips Electronics, and Network Computer.[18]

With the proliferation of devices that provide access to AOL
Anywhere, the company has to deliver content everywhere.

That's a key driver in AOL's association with Time Warner, which includes numerous new and extended cooperative agreements (that were largely ignored when they were announced at the same time as the blockbuster merger plan). Among these are alliances that venture into largely uncharted territory; for example, AOL members gain access to Time Warner promotional music clips, broadband CNN news content is distributed on the "AOL Plus" service available to subscribers with broadband connections, and AOL will deliver instant messaging, MovieFone, and other brands on Time Warner's Road Runner broadband cable service (which itself is a five-way joint venture that includes Compaq Computer and Microsoft).[19]

Alliances and acquisitions can also provide the wherewithal – otherwise lacking or perhaps too risky – to step into entirely new business realms.

Alliances can be an ideal vehicle for companies to enter new markets and lines of business because they:

- spread the risk of new ventures among two or more companies;

- can speed time to market to an extent that no company working alone could match; and

- tap the cumulative expertise and creativity of numerous firms required to adapt complex technologies functionally in practical products.

CASH IN ON THE VALUE YOU'VE BUILT

Today's blockbuster acquisitions by new-economy companies such as AOL – of which the Time Warner deal is prominent for its size and symbolism, but otherwise an almost everyday occurrence – are largely made possible by sky-high stock-market valuations. Investors have in effect turned shares into a form of currency that doesn't merely permit acquisitions, but almost requires them as one of the few ways that companies can realize tangible current gain from soaring valuations. "These high valuations are partly based on the assumption that companies can translate their high stock prices [via mergers and takeovers] into real revenue and earnings before people get impatient," says venture capitalist Keith Benjamin.[20]

But a stratospheric market valuation is only one reflection – and, ultimately, not a widely conferred one – of a company's value. Far more common among firms of all types is the often less tangible value of the information and insight it has about its customers, and the standing of its brands and its very name in the minds of consumers. As the runaway leader among Internet service providers, AOL has masterfully cashed in on this sort of value in the form of alliances and cooperative agreements with other companies. "[T]wo years ago, AOL execs were shoveling out millions to get content to come to them," *Time* reported in 1997. "Now Case is often the one cashing checks."[21]

Among AOL's deals predicated on the value of its franchise at about that time: Preview Travel paid to become AOL's online travel agent, 1-800-FLOWERS became the cyberflorist, and – in a double play – Amazon bought rights to sell books on the aol.com Website, while Barnes & Noble shelled out to become

AN EARLY VICTORY WITH TEL-SAVE[23]

One of the first deals by which AOL began to translate the value of the franchise it had built into cold cash was struck in 1997 with a then-unknown company called Tel-Save – now known as Talk.com. The start-up was launched after the break-up of AT&T by "tough-talking entrepreneur" Dan Borislow, who not only possessed the moxie to launch a business reselling long-distance phone service to consumers, but decided he would market it via a single, essentially unproven medium – the Internet – and, more specifically, AOL.

Borislow introduced himself to AOL's Bob Pittman by saying he had a $50 million check in his pocket to exchange for an agreement under which Tel-Save would become an exclusive marketer of long-distance service to AOL subscribers. Borislow's value proposition to those folks was based on wringing as much cost as possible out of providing toll phone service, chiefly by doing away with paper-based transactions – marketing and billing – and conducting those exchanges online instead.

Although AOL had previously discussed alliance with AT&T and Sprint, Pittman had the insight to conclude he should cast AOL's lot with Tel-Save. The result was a three-year deal and $100 million paid to AOL, along with Tel-Save warrants and a potential share of profits.

Today's Talk.com boasts annual revenues of $500 million, and Borislow boasts that the deal with AOL "actually created billions of dollars in market value" in AOL and Web portals such as Yahoo,

> with which he made subsequent deals. "I think that was a stimulus for the whole e-commerce business."
>
> That's boastful, but possibly not far off the mark, based on comments by David Colburn, who led negotiations with Borislow for AOL: "The deal said that this is a real medium that can generate major dollars – that online is a very special marketplace and that AOL can make money."

the exclusive book retailer inside AOL.[22]

As AOL's value has continued to soar, the company has continued to squeeze maximum value from its clout with customers, for example, in the form of partnerships with Wal-Mart, Circuit City, and Blockbuster video. "Those alliances bring traditional retailers oft-touted new customers and marketing opportunities," *The Los Angeles Times* comments. "What's more, the partnerships offer bricks-and-mortar retailers a whole range of new business opportunities on the Internet, which not that long ago seemed to have left them in the dust." And AOL further derives a clout-begets-clout boost from the deals, the *Times* notes: "The portals are able to push their products to customers who may not yet be connected online – as well as leverage store services and employees to allay the concerns of newer computer users."[24]

... OR HESITATE TO SLEEP WITH THE ENEMY

Internet-related enterprise is often compared to the shoot-'em-up settling of the US "Wild West." But there's at least one significant absence in today's wired world: the bad guys wearing black hats. Now the firm you most love to hate one day can be your partner or buy-out target the next. That's only one of the new rules related to alliance and acquisition, which suggest you should:

- *Put Coke vs. Pepsi in a museum.* Rivalries that cross all bounds of time and business lines are largely a thing of the past. The demands imposed today by incessant, Internet-speed competition require the sort of flexibility demonstrated by AOL in acquiring CompuServe and partnering with Microsoft. Look for every opportunity to add to your resources – with current and former foes as well as friends.

- *Ally and buy to be everything you aren't.* Today's consumers – corporate and individual – increasingly look for single-source providers of a range of products, services, and expertise; gaps of any sort can be deadly. Steve Case recognized this emerging reality when AOL was barely able to stand on its own two feet, and found strength in partnerships and acquisitions. Increasingly, that's the way companies can get big quick.

- *Discover new worlds with partners and purchases.* Beyond mere corporate survival, there is today the emerging imperative to keep up with (or ahead of) new technologies and burgeoning knowledge. Even the largest and most pervasive global enterprises can't keep up alone – witness the challenges AOL faces in maintaining its prominence as the Web explodes with both content and devices with which to access it. An answer here, too, is found in buying and allying.

- *Cash in on the value you've built.* AOL has been accorded value of historic proportions by its shareholders and its customers as well. But the days when a company could wait patiently for tangible returns on its value gains are gone. Partnerships and purchases offer avenues for cashing in on the gains your hard work and success have earned.

NOTES

1. Matt Murray, Nikhil Deogun, and Nick Wingfield, "Can Time Warner Click With AOL?" *The Wall Street Journal*, January 14, 2000.

2. Jim Seymour, "Why AOL Will Be Just Fine, Thanks," *TheStreet.com*, May 25, 1999.

3. Uncredited, "AOL Discussing Unspecified Partnership With AT&T," *Los Angeles Times* (from Bloomberg News), March 9, 2000.

4. Bernard Wysocki Jr, "More Companies Cut Risk by Collaborating With Their 'Enemies,'" *The Wall Street Journal*, January 31, 2000.

5. Jared Sandberg, "America Online Stars in Soap-opera-like Internet Action," *The Wall Street Journal*, March 18, 1996.

6. Jared Sandberg, "America Online Stars in Soap-opera-like Internet Action," *The Wall Street Journal*, March 18, 1996.

7. Bernard Wysocki Jr, "More Companies Cut Risk by Collaborating With Their 'Enemies,'" *The Wall Street Journal*, January 31, 2000.

8. Compiled from numerous reports.

9. Mark Potts, "America Online Serves a Growing Market of Home Computer Users," *The Washington Post*, July 27, 1992.

10. Mark Lewyn, "For America Online, Nothing Is as Nice as a Niche," *Business Week*, September 14, 1992.

11. Daniel Southerland, "America Online's Rapid Rise," *The Washington Post*, November 8, 1993.

12. Jared Sandberg, "America Online Stars in Soap-opera-like Internet Action," *The Wall Street Journal*, March 18, 1996.

13. John Simons, "Steve Case Wants to Get America Online," *US News & World Report*, March 25, 1996.

14. Michael Krantz, "AOL, You've Got Netscape," *Time*, December 7, 1998.

15. Abigail Goldman, "Sears, Roebuck, AOL Announce Retail Alliance," *The Los Angeles Times*, March 15, 2000.

16. Mark Leibovich, "Steve Case Plods to the Vanguard of the Internet," *The Washington Post*, November 25, 1998.

17. Andrew Zajac, "Watch Out, Microsoft: AOL Opens Major Window to Cyberspace," *Chicago Tribune*, November 25, 1998.

18. Catherine Yang, "There's No Escaping AOL," *Business Week*, December 6, 1999.

19. AOL–Time Warner joint corporate news release.

20. William J. Holstein, *et al.* "You've Got a Deal!" *US News & World Report,* January 24, 2000.

21. Joshua Cooper Ramo, "How AOL Lost the Battles but Won the War," *Time,* September 22, 1997.

22. Marc Gunther, "The Internet Is Mr. Case's Neighborhood," *Fortune,* March 30, 1998.

23. Marc Gunther, "The Internet Is Mr. Case's Neighborhood," *Fortune,* March 30, 1998; CNNfn television network, "Entrepreneurs Only," November 12, 1999.

24. Abigail Goldman, "Sears, Roebuck, AOL Announce Retail Alliance," *The Los Angeles Times,* March 15, 2000.

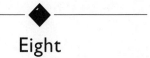

Eight

LEVERAGE SUCCESSES, BUILD YOUR BRANDS

IN THIS CHAPTER

There's not much exaggeration in saying AOL's super success is built on nothing, because the company started with next to nothing. Looking back, it's clear that Steve Case made something from nothing in an incremental, stair-step fashion: Offer a product customers will want; market it like mad to attract them; use customer numbers to attract advertisers; cross-sell customers to added offerings; build the brand identity of those offerings; use the range of offerings to attract still more customers. Here is Professor Case's textbook example of making a corporate mountain from a molehill of resources.

---

66 "Case Enterprises' main business was essentially a marketing scheme based on a paper route," according to *Newsweek*, referring to the boyhood business ventures of Steve Case and brother Dan. "Steve used his access to the neighbors' homes to peddle everything from seeds to watches to personalized Christmas cards."[1]

Thus, it appears, Steve Case learned early lessons in the power of leverage – building multiple lines of business from a single, perhaps shaky, endeavor; selling those who bought one product on the need for your other products; building a name for yourself and your offerings. Those lessons would serve him well enough to rocket AOL from lagging weakling to global powerhouse in less than 10 years.

MAKE YOUR OFFERINGS ESSENTIAL TO CUSTOMERS

Think through the short list of the most successful products of the past hundred years or so and you'll find necessities where there were once only wants. The telephone and automobile, for example, were wanted but not needed in the early 1900s. In relatively short order, though, consumers came to regard them as essential – and AT&T, GM, and Ford were soon listed among the world's largest corporations.

Jump to the recent past, and consider *The New York Times*' account of "how Steve Case turned America Online from laughable to extraordinary": "… just follow a typical suburban teenager after school. You'll see that e-mail and chat rooms are as important to his social system as cruising the mall and talking on the phone."[2]

AOL charges a fee, and hardly a token one, for content and services that, with a little effort, can largely be had at no cost. But still the company adds subscribers.

Thereby arises necessity from want, and AOL inches ever closer to its mission of building "a global medium as *essential* to people's lives as the telephone and the television" – emphasis added.[3] What's essential is habit-forming, a fact not lost on AOL executives such as Barry Schuler, who says, "The whole game is about building the online habit."[4]

That "habit" – in this age of limited attention spans and the TV-remote-enabled ability to surf through channels or the Net – is called "stickiness": attracting eyeballs to your content and keeping them there. On that score, AOL's success borders on phenomenal, as it has claimed its subscribers spend 80 percent of their online time inside the service (including time spent with content residing within AOL that's also available on the Web).[5]

That statistic, even if it's actually somewhat lower than claimed, is the cornerstone of the massive revenue-generating structure AOL has built upon it: from 20-some million subscribers paying 20-some dollars monthly; advertisers paying hundreds of millions more to reach those folks, and so forth. "The whole key to where the profits are is keeping people within the AOL playpen," says University of Illinois professor Robert McChesney.[6]

And no single toy within that playpen has so occupied people as chat – the online activity that most differentiated AOL from its early competitors (and, ironically, may be the least essential in fact, but most essential as perceived by many customers). "Chat is addictive, and it's famous for keeping people online for long periods of time," according to a 1997 commentary in *Upside* magazine.[7] And, as Case and his team were smart enough to recognize, chat rooms organized by topic encourage users to self-segregate based on their special interests, conveniently exposing themselves to highly targeted advertising that AOL can sell at premium rates.

Yet another benefit flows from becoming essential in customers' minds: the ability to charge a premium without unacceptable attrition. Here, too, AOL has excelled. It charges a fee, and hardly a token one, for content and services that, with a little effort, can largely be had at no cost. But still the company adds subscribers, in part because so many people will pay to avoid "a little effort," and also (looking at the underside of the same coin) because those addictions to all AOL offers are hard to break. And most people require a considerable kick in the teeth – be it price hike, poor service, or whatever – to go to the trouble of switching to another provider. That's not the basis on which any business cares to retain customers, but at a minimum it can hold some of them long enough to prove it's worth staying after all.

HOW AOL GAVE NEW MEANING TO THE WORD "UBIQUITY" [8]

A corporate effort dubbed "AOL Anywhere" was launched in 1999, aimed at delivering all brands of AOL service to users no matter where they are or what sort of device they happen to be using. The idea is to make AOL ubiquitous.

Seven years earlier, AOL launched a now legendary marketing effort that might appropriately have been named "AOL Everywhere," because the company disgorged a seemingly endless stream of computer diskettes with software for a free trial on AOL service. The idea for the campaign is attributed to AOL marketing chief Jan Brandt, whose similar campaign for the *My Weekly Reader* book club was based on sending prospects a free book instead of the traditional four-page pitch letter.

From 1992 to 1996, any American with a name and fixed address would have been hard pressed to escape AOL's carpet-bombing campaign. "My job was to give new meaning to the word ubiquity," says Brandt. That included diskettes enclosed with boxes of cereal, music CDs, flash-frozen steaks, in-flight airline meals, and an issue of *Reform Judaism* magazine, among thousands of other channels. In all, some 250 million diskettes were shoveled into consumers' hands.

The effort was costly. Aside from outlays of vast sums, AOL got in considerable hot water with investors and regulators for the legal but misleading way it accounted for marketing costs, generated a "churn rate" of subscriber sign-ups and quick cancellation that would embarrass a door-to-door magazine subscription salesman, and attracted more service samplers than its infrastructure could handle (*recounted in the next chapter*).

But the effort was also cost-effective. Ten percent of the diskettes distributed were used for a free trial – an exceptional acceptance rate for any sort of direct marketing. Subscriber numbers vaulted from less than 200,000 when the campaign started to more than 5 million when it tailed off in 1996. And rocketing customer rolls were a chief reason that investors perceived a bright future for AOL, thus bidding up the stock price and providing the financial wherewithal for the company to acquire and invest in the many other companies, which would provide the talent and technologies that further boosted future prospects.

The campaign was curtailed by now-president and COO Bob Pittman, who correctly perceived that AOL was sufficiently established as a brand to shift marketing to a more traditional mix of various media. As a result, over the two years from 1996 to 1998, AOL's cost of acquiring a new subscriber, after accounting for those who don't stick with the service, fell from about $375 to $75, according to a *New York Times* account. And the churn rate – cancellations soon after the free trial expires – dropped from 75 percent to 40 percent.

MAKE YOUR CUSTOMERS ESSENTIAL FOR OTHERS' OFFERINGS

Time Inc. built a media empire that was the envy of its age. *Time* magazine grew from 9,000 circulation in the year of its founding, 1923, to one million by the early 1940s and a peak of 4.6 million in the early 1980s.[9]

"That, of course, is horse-and-buggy stuff compared with what's going on in the Internet world these days," *The Wall Street Journal* comments. "[AOL] had about one million users in 1994. Powered by the Internet explosion, that has multiplied about 20-fold."

And AOL's Bob Pittman, with a depth of perception to match Steve Case's, plus the executive ability to turn it into cold cash, would squeeze value from Net users as no one else has yet. By late 1997, *Money* magazine recounts:

> "More people were logging on to AOL than were tuning in to MTV. On the strength of that audience, Pittman was able to start cutting big advertising deals, like the $100 million, multi-year commitment the service got from long-distance provider Tel-Save [*see 'An Early Victory With Tel-Save' in the previous chapter*]. Revenues hit $1.7 billion in 1997, up 70 percent ... The company still had scant earnings, but its market cap swelled to $9.2 billion."[10]

With a prime-time audience rivaling those of top cable TV programs – folks whose income and affluence demographics could make ad buyers lick their chops – plus accelerating numbers in terms of both numbers of users and average time they spent online, Pittman started racking up big deals with retailers of travel, flowers, music, loans, and a host of other products.[11]

Retailers increasingly find they can't afford not to be on AOL, a circumstance dramatically illustrated by the story of interactive games company Kesmai, which was displaced on AOL by an AOL-owned games company, resulting within weeks in 92 percent fewer people using Kesmai's games. Pittman is a master in wielding clout of such proportions; news accounts report that he'll cut deals that often provide multiple income streams for AOL, sometimes extending years into the future.[12]

So AOL's presumed future direction for boosting the price of wooing its subscribers consists of a two-pronged effort:

- Attract more eyeballs – boosting subscriber numbers for the flagship Internet service and the growing family of brands such as Netscape and ICQ.

- Keep users online longer – far past the average 63 minutes daily claimed by AOL's corporate data in early 2000.

More folks exposed more often to AOL content means more advertisers are likely to conclude that presence on AOL is essential, even at Pittman's prices.

WEAVE A WEB OF CROSS-MARKETING

AOL is seizing the opportunities that arise from having more customers than any of its direct competitors and more sellers who want to reach those people with their own advertising messages. "Because they have so many customers, they can sell more products and services to them," says Edward A. Bennett, who previously headed AOL competitor Prodigy.[13]

It's a virtuous upward spiral – success begets success; everyone loves a winner, and so forth – so long as the subscribers at the foundation of the process believe they're getting value in exchange for their contribution to AOL's bottom line.

And with the official AOL–Time Warner union looming, it's probably safe to say that the cross-marketing to come will make anything in the past look like teenagers Steve and Dan Case pushing Swiss watches on their paper-route customers. At events surrounding the mega-merger announcement, Case and Gerald Levin repeatedly mentioned the "synergies" to be gained as one product boosts another and vice versa, in almost limitless combinations of cross-promotion, product tie-ins, and other marketing maneuvers. Such opportunities were noted by *US News & World Report* in a manner that perhaps looked askance at its rival news magazine:

> "Even before AOL consummated its deal, *Time* magazine was using its cover to promote the movies 'Eyes Wide Shut' and 'Pokémon: The First Movie,' which were produced by – guess who? – Time Warner. The AOL–Time Warner deal raised the prospect that *Time* or *Fortune* or CNN would be increasingly tempted to promote AOL's vision of the future, but not, say, Microsoft's or AT&T's."[14]

For his part, Case has more than once termed other such conjectures "silly," and journalists and executives both within and competing against the nascent media colossus have publicly expressed opinions that generally concur. Perhaps the main challenge for Case, Levin, and their team will be determining the dividing line between synergistic and inappropriate.

It's a not-altogether unpleasant challenge, stemming as it does from a
position of incredible strength.
And – in this age of accelerating
consolidation and partnerships –
one that many executives will increasingly face in the future. "It's all
about leverage," AOL's Barry Schuler
accurately observes. "End of discussion."[15]

> "It's all about leverage. End of discussion."
> – AOL executive Barry Schuler

Well, not quite end of discussion. Because any company of any kind is leveraging its relationship with its customers – or had better be in an environment of shrinking margins and custom-ers' instant access to providers around the world. Like AOL, the provider's constant quest today must be for an ever-increas-ing "share of customer," selling more to the people you're selling to already.

BRANDS SEND MESSAGES – MANAGE THEM[16]

AOL's master brand builder, Bob Pittman, understands and respects the power of brands to send messages, as does Richard Gerstman, president of New York City brand identity and design marketing firm Interbrand Gerstman + Meyers. "There is a message behind every brand, whether or not you manage the brand and control the message that consumers get from it," Gerstman says.

He offers these examples to demonstrate some of the key characteristics of messages conveyed by brands:

- *British Airways*

  Research indicated that the company was generally seen as too formal, arrogant, and even cold. This was far from management's stated objective of being seen as approachable, global, and caring. So a complete overhaul of the brand extended from repainting planes to retraining front-line employees. "The new focus was on British Airways as a citizen of the world, bringing the world's people together," Gerstman recounts. "Artists from around the world were commissioned to create a variety of airplane tail designs. But new design was carried across everything associated with the airline, from terminals to ticket folders." Result: "Research shows that people think of British Airways as more caring and customer-focused."

- *Mead Johnson*

  The company was identified narrowly in consumers' minds with only two products: Enfamil formula for babies and Sustacal nutrition drink for the elderly. "The objective was to gain identification with products for people of any age." So branding redesign focused on two changes: the addition of a word to the trade name, to become Mead Johnson Nutritionals, and a new brand icon based on the mathematical symbol for infinity (which looks like the numeral 8 on its side). "The message conveyed in this redesign," Gerstman comments, "is that Mead Johnson products contribute to the consumer's good health throughout the life cycle – from cradle to grave."

CAPITALIZE ON BRAND POWER

"Brands win," says AOL president and COO Bob Pittman, and that means AOL wins. "Consider these pairs," *Forbes* magazine suggests:

> "'Fights cavities' – Crest; 'Natural' – Thom's of Maine; 'Fresh breath' – Closeup. Like these toothpaste companies, AOL has built a brand. Sure, it took some magical accounting and passing out more trial disks and CD-ROMs than the number of joints smoked at Woodstock, but when you hear 'online service' you think 'AOL.' This brand awareness isn't going away."[17]

Similarly, *TheStreet.com* comments, "For many Americans, 'AOL' is nearly a synonym for both 'the Web' and 'e-mail.' "[18] And *Fortune* quoted "a disgruntled content provider" who implicitly praised in saying, "Pittman wants to build one brand, and that's AOL."[19]

Bad news for the disgruntled content provider: AOL's fixation on building its brands has only intensified. When AOL announced its purchase of Netscape and partnership with Sun Microsystems, *The Chicago Tribune* noted, "the press release announcing the ... deals uses variations of the word 'brand' 21 times in fewer than five pages, including the headline, 'AOL to operate most popular and diverse family of brands in cyberspace.' "[20]

What's the value in building a brand? Aside from the hardly inconsiderable benefit of having customers think of your company as synonymous with its products, there's this observation from Bob Pittman: "I remind people all the time that Coca-

Cola does not win the taste test. Microsoft is not the best operating system. Brands win."[21]

LEVERAGE SUCCESSES, BUILD YOUR BRANDS

There's no more smooth sailing or slacking off in business today – achieving success means redoubling your effort to
maintain and extend success. Like AOL, you've got to bear
down and:

- *Make your offerings essential to customers.* A customer who isn't
  committed to you is only a buyer, likely to be here today,
  gone tomorrow. AOL has written into its very mission that it
  will become "essential" to its users – and has gone out and
  made it happen. That's the model for any company that
  wants to last in the 21st century.

- *Make your customers essential for others' offerings.* AOL's first significant accomplishment in extending its franchise beyond
  customers was to begin building significant, long-term revenue from advertisers willing to pay handsomely for a crack
  at the millions on AOL. Successful companies have tremendous – and often untapped – value in the loyal customers
  they've won. AOL shows how to squeeze critical cash flow
  from people who've come to rely on you.

- *Weave a web of cross-marketing.* Why settle for a small share of
  business from the customer who only cherry-picks from your
  product lines? AOL understands and acts on the business
  wisdom asserting that your best prospect is your current customer – provided you tell him about your other offerings.

- *Capitalize on brand power.* It's said there's magic in brands, and AOL demonstrates as well as any company its supreme wizardry when it comes to building brands. The take-home lesson here: You can't spend too much time creating an identity in customers' minds between your products and your brands.

NOTES

1. Jared Sandberg, "Case Study," *Newsweek*, January 24, 2000.

2. Saul Hansell, "Now, AOL Everywhere," *The New York Times*, July 4, 1999.

3. Speech at National Press Club, Federal News Service transcript, October 26, 1998.

4. Saul Hansell, "Now, AOL Everywhere," *The New York Times*, July 4, 1999.

5. Joshua Cooper Ramo, "How AOL Lost the Battles but Won the War," *Time*, September 22, 1997.

6. William J. Holstein, *et al.*, "You've Got a Deal!" *US News & World Report*, January 24, 2000.

7. Curt Monash and Linda Barlow, "AOL Doesn't Suck!" *Upside*, May 1997.

8. Saul Hansell, "America Online's Triumvirate in Cyberspace," *The New York Times*, February 16, 1998; Marc Gunther, "The Internet Is Mr. Case's Neighborhood," *Fortune*, March 30,

1998; David Akin, "The Winner's Case: Steve Case Has overcome Many Setbacks," *The National Post*, November 25, 1998; Charles H. Ferguson, *High Stakes, No Prisoners*, Times Business, New York, 1999.

9. Martin Peers, Nick Wingfield, and Laura Landro, "AOL and Time Warner Leap Boundaries to Join in Mammoth Merger," *The Wall Street Journal*, January 11, 2000.

10. John Helyar, "If You Want to Understand What's Happened to the Stock Market in the Past Three Years Just Look at America Online," *Money*, October 1999.

11. Saul Hansell, "America Online's Triumvirate in Cyberspace," *The New York Times*, February 16, 1998.

12. Marc Gunther, "The Internet Is Mr. Case's Neighborhood," *Fortune*, March 30, 1998.

13. Saul Hansell, "Now, AOL Everywhere," *The New York Times*, July 4, 1999.

14. William J. Holstein, *et al.*, "You've Got a Deal!" *US News & World Report*, January 24, 2000.

15. Marc Gunther, "The Internet Is Mr. Case's Neighborhood," *Fortune*, March 30, 1998.

16. Author interview.

17. Guy Kawasaki, "Get Off Steve's Case," *Forbes*, January 27, 1997.

18. Jim Seymour, "Why AOL Will Be Just Fine, Thanks," *TheStreet.com*, May 25, 1999.

19. Marc Gunther, "The Internet Is Mr. Case's Neighborhood," *Fortune*, March 30, 1998.

20. Andrew Zajac, "Watch Out, Microsoft: AOL Opens Major Window to Cyberspace," *Chicago Tribune*, November 25, 1998.

21. Marc Gunther, "The Internet Is Mr. Case's Neighborhood," *Fortune*, March 30, 1998.

Nine

ADMIT MISTAKES AND GROW FORWARD

IN THIS CHAPTER

AOL, though only a teenager in years, has made or been charged with enough mistakes to fill the life of a centenarian. Countless press accounts have reported the company's travails – sometimes with more than a hint of glee – and scores of commentators have served as judge, jury, and hangman in condemning the firm to death. But few, if any, reports have considered this critical question: would AOL have attained its current size, stature, and success if it had been managed to avoid its many missteps and crises? The answer: Almost certainly not. This chapter considers the ways in which AOL's history reveals that mistakes are often inseparable from taking risks, growing aggressively, and leading the pack.

There are elements of the Keystone Kops, Indiana Jones, and the Perils of Pauline in AOL's history, *The Wall Street Journal* observes. "From its beginnings, in fact, AOL has veered from one crisis to another in a way that has terrified and fascinated observers."[1] Yet AOL, like a cat with nine lives, has survived and, improbable as it may seem, succeeded beyond the wildest dreams of anyone, perhaps, but Steve Case.

Case apparently understood from AOL's Day One the business implications of a venerable adage: To make an omelet, you've gotta' break some eggs.

RECOGNIZE THAT RISK WITHOUT STUMBLING IS PARALYSIS

Some measure of risk is familiar to just about all of us: A person might walk outside any day and be flattened by a truck. But Steve Case has run AOL in a way that puts risk on a roller coaster – and seems almost to dare it to take him down. This is perhaps not too surprising, considering that here's a guy who decided to chuck his relatively secure marketing career at a young age and risk his future in an ill-defined industry that then lacked even the technology to make it commercially viable. When you've cast your lot with something that risky, subsequent gambles – such as slamming the door on an unsubtle offer from Bill Gates – may not feel like corporate life-or-death matters.

> "Individuals and corporations must cope with an economy in which both risks and rewards are escalating."
> – The High-Risk Society

That's certainly the impression Case has conveyed to those who've observed him over time – and that demeanor has served AOL well. *Newsweek* seems on target in saying, "AOL survived in part because Case was able to convey his quiet confidence to jittery customers, and because he was able to move more quickly and decisively to fix problems than his corporate competitors."[2]

Those traits are perhaps a necessity for a firm that provides Internet access – a risky line of work to say the least. Yet Case has seemed intent on compounding the inherent risks with his own decisions. Prime example: Timing of AOL's conversion from subscriber fees based on time spent online to flat-rate monthly fees for unlimited use. "The results were predictable," *Fortune* reported. "Customers spent more time online; systems overloaded; users felt justifiably betrayed..."[3]

Although such facts regarding what *happened* appear to leave no argument for what AOL did, the advisability of the company's action can be fully evaluated only by also considering what *didn't happen*. That is, might an AOL that decided to hang on to its time-based pricing until capacity was increased have lost a critical mass of subscribers to less costly services?

Such considerations are not mere academic exercises, particularly in today's Internet-speed economy, as Michael J. Mandel substantiates in his book *The High-Risk Society*. Yes, he allows, until recent times, most people and companies enjoyed greater security and more reliable economic advances. But he cites also the often neglected downside of those more placid years: The more dramatic economic advances that are commonplace today were almost unheard of then.

"Individuals and corporations must cope with an economy in which both risks and rewards are escalating," Mandel writes. "[They] would like to run from uncertainty. But they cannot. In the 1990s and beyond, many of the best routes to success require even greater risk."[4]

AOL AS CRISIS CENTRAL – THEN AND NOW[5]

Although AOL seems to have careened from one goof to another since birth, 1996 unquestionably takes the prize as the firm's Year of Living Dangerously. It was marked by these nightmares:

- It settled a class action lawsuit filed by subscribers who claimed they were overcharged for service. Prosecutors in nearly 40 states had threatened to sue AOL for what they called questionable billing methods.
- Superstar FedEx exec William Razzouk – brought in to bring some calm and order to the company – arrived as AOL's new president and abruptly departed only four months later, under cover of the all-purpose corporate excuse: to pursue other opportunities.
- In August an overstrained technological infrastructure gave out under the weight of too much use and too little capacity – causing a worldwide shutdown for 19 hours and making AOL's travails page 1 news.
- In October, the company abandoned its legal but highly criticized practice of booking its marketing costs as capital expenses amortized over two years – absorbing the hit from a one-time $385 million charge to write down the outstanding expenses that it had yet to amortize. It reverted to the more common practice of reporting the costs as expenses when they're incurred.

Problems haven't since flown at AOL quite so fast and furious. But the company still finds itself in hot water often enough:

- In December 1999, the company canceled its subscribers' long-standing instructions to suppress its famous pop-up ads, thus forcing those customers to again go to the trouble of reconfirming their wish to be pop-up free or once again have to contend with the ad gimmick.

- About the same time, AOL issued a version 5.0 of its flagship Internet service software that, with specific answers from users during installation, will rewrite a computer's settings for connection to the Internet such that the computer automatically connects to AOL whenever the user goes online. At the same time, it disables the network configurations that provide Internet access through other service providers.

AOL's explanations for the actions are reasonable: It's an effort to extend their widely appreciated simplicity and it's no different from what other providers' installation software also does. But criticism falls most heavily on an industry heavyweight – and AOL is one of the heaviest.

LOOK PAST PREDICTIONS OF DOOM TO "PRETTY GOOD" ODDS

Steve Case is accustomed to taking risks that not only are regarded as foolish by outside observers, but also are apparently viewed as long-shots by his own employees – as when, on hearing almost universal praise for the company's acquisition of CompuServe, they "shared a moment of collective corporate shock: 'Well, I guess Steve was right.' "[6]

Case may not have been surprised to be doubted by his own people, since he'd long since grown accustomed to having industry observers prejudge his every move as a sure-fire failure. And they may be forgiven for doing so, *Fortune* intimated, given that Case had "outsmarted just about every media and communications giant pursuing the holy grail of interactivity." Considering that ventures undertaken by powerhouses such as Bell Atlantic, Time Warner, MCI, AT&T, and Microsoft had fizzled or failed, "What were the odds that from that crowd Steve Case would emerge as the winner?" The answer: "Case always thought the odds were pretty good."[7]

"I was the one who two years ago said, 'Bye-bye, AOL.' What they have done is extraordinary."
– C-Net chairman Halsey Minor

If the AOL story was a motion picture, the Tinseltown dream factory would write an ending in which all those who doubted Case through the years would by now have come around to awe-struck agreement with the CEO's view of which risks are worth taking. But that only happens in the picture show. In real life, AOL deconstructors are still at work, contending the company has definitely committed what will prove to be its fatal blunder *this* time.

Shortly after the AOL–Time Warner merger was announced, for example, Wall Street and Silicon Valley chronicler Michael Lewis (*The New, New Thing*), in a *Wall Street Journal* article titled "AOL: Almost Obscenely Large," derided the world's biggest merger by noting that, "In a stroke AOL has lowered its credit rating, acquired thousands of journalists and movie executives whose talent is getting attention rather than making money, and transformed itself from a sexy, fast-growing company beloved by the current stock market into a dull, slow-moving one the market is likely to disdain." A key lesson of the Internet boom, Lewis writes, is that "it's riskier than ever to be a big, deeply entrenched company … The bigger AOL becomes, … the harder it will be for the company to adapt."[8]

Lewis's outlook may prove accurate. If it does, a gigabyte of credit goes to him – the first person to forecast AOL's fall and get it right. On the other hand, events to date strongly predict that Lewis may someday be in the same position as C-Net chairman Halsey Minor, who admitted in 1999, "I was the one who two years ago said, 'Bye-bye, AOL.' What they have done is extraordinary. They have created a great business."[9]

AOL, AKA:[10]

Through its mistakes and the disdain it has drawn from Net heads who look down on its decidedly uncool products, AOL has earned derisive nicknames such as these:

- America on Hold – particularly when its aggressive marketing and switch to flat-rate pricing produced use it was unprepared to handle.
- The Kmart Network – indicating what the digerati viewed as a lack of sophistication.
- The Internet on Training Wheels – for the same reason.
- The McDonald's of Cyberspace – again, for the same reason, but with an unintended compliment, given the fast-food chain's walloping market share and global reach.
- The Cockroach of Cyberspace – probably the most appropriate of the names listed here, which AOL earned for its incredible ability to survive again and again in the face of crises that would seemingly have brought down any enterprise.

GO FOR GROWTH – ACCEPT THE GOOFS

Recalling AOL's supposedly blunder-filled past, *Wall Street Journal* columnist Holman W. Jenkins Jr laments, "The worst journalistic mistake we ever made was writing about America Online instead of buying the stock. The occasion was the unprecedented outpouring of recrimination after AOL switched to flat-rate pricing in late 1996. Users suddenly had no reason to be parsimonious with their usage. The busy signal became the national anthem. A cry went up for the head of Steve Case." And every dollar invested in AOL stock at that time, Jenkins adds, is worth $70 today.[11]

Jenkins is but one expert confounded by AOL's continuing, seemingly inexorable growth in the face of an almost endless stream of adversity. "They have flourished despite a series of technical problems," admits David Cassel, editor of a Website called AOL Watch, which links to free sign-ups for competing Internet services. His explanation for the company's success: "AOL is a triumph of Steve Case's marketing skills."[12]

Also count mutual fund manager David Tice in the incredulous camp. Tice started "shorting" AOL stock – betting it would fall in price – in 1996, on grounds the company's reported profits were illusory. When the firm bowed to public pressure and altered the way it booked marketing costs – incurring a one-time charge that more than wiped out all of its previous reported profits – Tice's view seemed prescient. But AOL stock subsequently didn't suffer; it soared. Two months after the supposed accounting debacle, Tice was forced by AOL's climbing stock value to put up almost $100,000 to cover his short position. He concludes, "We were right on the accounting issue, but Wall Street didn't care."[13]

"There has been plenty of reason to believe the forecasts of doom" for AOL, *Business Week* commented in early 1996, just *before* the series of events described nearby under the heading "AOL as Crisis Central – Then and Now." "Ever since 1993, when the company launched the bold drive for market share that has brought it to this point, naysayers have predicted that Case would falter and AOL spin out of control."[14]

> "Honesty, apology, contrition. What could people say? ... AOL and Case won big points on the reputation front..."
> – *Total Exposure: Controlling Your Company's Image in the Glare of the Business Media Explosion*

What accounts for growth in the face of presumed blunders? Jenkins is certainly right about Steve Case's marketing skills, as is *Time*'s 1997 observation that "Case is at least one step ahead of the complaints."[15] But perhaps a more penetrating explanation is found by inverting the implicit cause and effect of the question: Growth may not have occurred in spite of blunders. Instead, blunders may be a mostly unavoidable byproduct of soaring growth.

That contention is supported, at least implicitly, in the findings of research such as that conducted in the 1990s by management consultants Dwight L. Gertz and Joao P.A. Baptista and reported in their book *Grow to Be Great: Breaking the Downsizing Cycle*. They examined characteristics of growth in some 1,000 large companies and found repeatedly that growth experiences of companies contradict many of business's least challenged beliefs. For example, their studies revealed that a focus on growing revenues and profits brings better returns than a focus on cost cutting.[16]

Miscalculations may also be equally a byproduct of innovation, as Charles H. Ferguson opines in his Internet-wars book *High Stakes, No Prisoners*: "Because things are so new, you have to make a lot of guesses, and sometimes you miss."[17]

And the response when you miss? Own up, as business executive Gustav Carlson advises in recounting Steve Case's response to AOL's famous infrastructure inadequacies of 1996, in his book *Total Exposure: Controlling Your Company's Image in the Glare of the Business Media Explosion*:

> "[Case] did not hide. Instead, he appeared in an advertising campaign designed specifically to deal with the problem. Yes, he told viewers and readers, the company had fallen behind the demand for its services and was scrambling to increase its capacity. That would probably take a few months. Sorry for the inconvenience. Thanks for your patience. Honesty, apology, contrition. What could people say? ... AOL and Case won big points on the reputation front, turning a near disaster into a public relations coup. And the company is reaping the benefits today."[18]

The AOL experience, then, confirms the advisability of, first, barreling full speed ahead for continuing growth and innovation, being prepared for unavoidable miscues, and expressing genuine regret and determination to make things better when mistakes are made.

ADMIT MISTAKES AND GROW FORWARD

AOL's many stumbles along its path to Internet ubiquity have provided grist for the mills of countless analysts, reporters,

THE BRIGHT SIDE OF BLUNDERS

Steve Case, who can probably see the bright side of an Edgar Allan Poe short story, found a hopeful sign in the 1996 overloading of AOL's inadequate infrastructure and resulting consumer outcry that some observers said would bring down the company: "What was happening, for really the first time, was that we impacted people's daily lives in a significant way," he says, apparently without intended irony.[19]

Case may be onto something, because the AOL experience suggests these not unfavorable conclusions can sometimes be derived from miscues and crises:

- *You're human.*
  We all make mistakes, and we occasionally enjoy the company of others who do the same.
- *You can be a hero.*
  Customer behavior studies indicate that people whose problems with a product or service are fixed right may afterward be counted among a company's staunchest supporters.
- *You're a hot ticket.* A crisis caused by demand for your product that you're unable to meet, *à la* Pokémon, may trigger even more demand.
- *You're at center stage.*
  It's been said that the only bad publicity is no publicity. Truer in Hollywood, perhaps, than on Wall Street, but there's still something to be said for being on the tip of every tongue.
- *You push the envelope.*
  Professional race car drivers involved in crashes get as much coverage as the guys who win the races. The trick is to survive – and soak in the admiration.

- *You're trying.*
  Don Quixote is loved for his "glorious quest"; AOL is admired for taking a stab at what others assume is impossible.
- *You sometimes beat the odds.*
  How many times has AOL attempted to do something that would have earned it scathing criticism for being so foolish – except that it worked?

observers, and hangers-on. But glitches and miscalculations are part and parcel of any firm's journey to the top of its business; the alternative course isn't only no mistakes, but no progress as well. That's why any corporate leader must:

- *Recognize that risk without stumbling is paralysis.* There's always a downside to any risky move; without it there's no risk – and no reward for making the effort. AOL has incurred the downside in many of its actions – publicly and famously so. But just as clearly, although often with far less public notice, it has reaped huge rewards for having shouldered risk and hit its targets. That's the payoff for any company in taking reasonable risk.

- *Look past predictions of doom to "pretty good" odds.* If your business vision is to turn dust devils into gold bricks, find another line of work. But if you've got an idea that meets your every test of logic and reasonableness, the moves that others see as high-risk gambles can in fact be well grounded execution of sensible strategies.

- *Go for growth – accept the goofs.* "Nobody's perfect," we all say, almost reflexively, from time to time. Yet there's news value, and often entertainment value as well, in the blunders by companies with the considerable public presence of an AOL. The corporate response could be to shy from bold moves and grow at a more leisurely pace. But in the competitive environment of the 21st century, that could well be a goof of fatal dimensions.

NOTES

1. Kara Swisher, "How Steve Case Morphed Into a Media Mogul," *The Wall Street Journal*, January 11, 2000.

2. Jared Sandberg, "Case Study," *Newsweek*, January 24, 2000.

3. Marc Gunther, "The Internet Is Mr. Case's Neighborhood," *Fortune*, March 30, 1998.

4. Michael J. Mandel, *The High-Risk Society: Peril & Promise in the New Economy*, Times Books, New York, 1997.

5. Compiled from numerous reports.

6. Joshua Cooper Ramo, "How AOL Lost the Battles but Won the War," *Time*, September 22, 1997.

7. Marc Gunther, "The Internet Is Mr. Case's Neighborhood," *Fortune*, March 30, 1998.

8. Michael Lewis, "AOL: Almost Obscenely Large," *The Wall Street Journal*, January 13, 2000.

9. Saul Hansell, "Now, AOL Everywhere," *The New York Times*, July 4, 1999.

10. Compiled from numerous reports.

11. Holman W. Jenkins Jr, "The Last Crazy Internet Valuation?" *The Wall Street Journal*, January 12, 2000.

12. Jon Swartz, "Case Study – A Look at Mr. America Online," *The San Francisco Chronicle*, February 22, 1999.

13. John Helyar, "If You Want to Understand What's Happened to the Stock Market in the Past Three Years Just Look at America Online," *Money*, October 1999.

14. Amy Cortese and Amy Barrett, "The Online World of Steve Case," *Business Week*, April 15, 1996.

15. Joshua Cooper Ramo, "How AOL Lost the Battles but Won the War," *Time*, September 22, 1997.

16. Author interview.

17. Charles H. Ferguson, *High Stakes, No Prisoners*, Times Business, New York, 1999.

18. Gustav Carlson, *Total Exposure: Controlling Your Company's Image in the Glare of the Business Media Explosion*, Amacom, New York, 2000.

19. Marc Gunther, "The Internet Is Mr. Case's Neighborhood," *Fortune*, March 30, 1998.

Ten

GET TO THE FUTURE TODAY

IN THIS CHAPTER

Our nostalgia for the past may be partly rooted in longing for change at a leisurely pace. The idea of being able to observe changed consumer behavior, analyze its implications, and respond to it appropriately with new products and services may be comforting; but it's also unrealistic. Information, commerce, and people all move too fast today to permit the sort of methodical R&D process we feel sure is required. Like it or not, we've got an Internet-speed world, and it makes the demands on all executives – handled so astutely by AOL's leaders – that are the subject of this chapter.

Hockey superstar Wayne Gretzky, asked to account for his ice-rink wizardry, said, "I skate to where the puck is going to be, not where it's been."

The Great One's assessment of his game, it would appear, is equally applicable to managing a business in current conditions. Just dare to go where consumers are right now – develop, test, and roll out the things those people need. By the time you're ready to deliver, they'll be somewhere else – and clamoring for features or services you can't provide.

So, like Gretzky, you've got to skate to where your target customers are going to be. With experience, insight, intuition, and a measure of fearlessness, you've got to look at where things stand today, figure out where they're heading, and be on the scene with the right solutions when they get there. It's the sort of daring accomplishment by which AOL has made its name.

BE WILLING TO BE WRONG –
FOR NOW

Much expert assessment of the planned AOL–Time Warner merger finds the proposed combination wanting. "The question is not why Time Warner would want to belong to AOL, but why AOL would want to own Time Warner, even at the market price," writes *The New, New Thing* author Michael Lewis in one of many commentaries critical of AOL's judgment. "A company whose share price has risen 800 times since 1992 has paid through the nose for a company nearly its own size whose share price has risen by barely five times."[1]

True enough – and long gone, receded into the distant past of yesterday, or perhaps five minutes ago. Either way, it's an assessment of what was. And that's not when the merger will take place – or prove its advisability. "Both companies are trading on prospects," says Steven Jones, a securities analyst with Value Line Inc., quoted in *The Christian Science Monitor*, which adds, "Those prospects include the enormous potential of Time Warner's millions of cable customers, who watch programs produced by its own Warner Brothers studios and news shows on CNN, which it also owns. In the future, analysts expect the companies to take advantage of the cable system that is in place to sell telephone services and higher-speed Internet connections." According to Jones, "They are one of the earliest businesses to meet this trend."[2]

In other words, AOL and Time Warner are ahead of the curve, the first couple to arrive at the much-anticipated Convergence Ball, making an entrance before the caterer is set up. If that's a *faux pas*, it's hardly Steve Case's first such transgression. "[Case] wasn't even on investors' radar screens until 1992," *US News & World Report* recounts. "Even then, when AOL went public, Case had trouble explaining to people what the company did. 'It was hard. People didn't quite get it.'"[3] How could they, when Case's business was barely grasped at the time by himself and a relative handful of geeks a continent away?

At that IPO moment, in early 1992, Case was possibly as wrong about proprietary online service as he may be about combining with Time Warner in early 2000. But he'd again gotten where consumers were heading before anyone else. AOL's subscriber base quintupled in two years and quintupled again in less than two more years. Case was at the entrance greeting every arrival (many of whom *still* "didn't quite get it," but didn't have to with AOL's ease of use). "The market changed overnight, and forever," *Time* magazine noted, reporting an event that may have taken everyone but Steve Case by surprise.[4]

> "[I]nvesting is not about poring over records of the past, but about projecting trends into the future."
> – *Wall Street Journal* columnist Holman W. Jenkins Jr

But even with AOL's steep subscriber-growth curve, Case was aware that relatively few people – eleven percent of Americans, far fewer worldwide, in 1996 – were online with AOL or anyone else. He reportedly looked for a model of growth to cable television, "which really only became an economically viable medium when it reached 20 percent or 30 percent of homes," according to *Business Week*. So Case, an admirer of cable-giant TCI's John C. Malone, embarked "on a Malone-like quest for market penetration. That's why he's punching AOL's accelerator now" – and thus, of course, incurred the predictable chorus of criticism from those who found every sort of fault in AOL's aggressive growth drive.[5]

So, to get back to the future, and how wrong AOL may be, based on *today's* circumstances, in yoking itself to Time Warner, the insight of business essayist Holman Jenkins may reflect the thinking at AOL headquarters: "Whether you are Warren Buffett or the wooliest Internet investor, investing is not about poring over records of the past, but about projecting trends into the future."[6]

That, of course, is just what smart investors and executives have always done – including, ironically, Time Inc. founders Henry Luce and Briton Hadden. "It is easy to forget in these breathless times that their original vision – a mass-appeal news and general-interest magazine for a national audience – was a New Thing of its day," claims *The Wall Street Journal*. "It was, in the words of Mr. Case's era, a first mover ... Some see what Mr. Case and his lieutenants are trying to do now as not much different."[7]

In other words, AOL is still willing to be wrong – as any company that wants to survive in the 21st century should be – until the world catches up.

AOL BUYS SOME TIME (WARNER)

A tidal wave of facts, quips, howls, and cheers followed announcement on January 10, 2000, of the planned AOL–Time Warner merger. Among them:

- "*Time* magazine was launched in 1923 by two Yale students, Henry Luce and Briton Hadden, and Warner Bros. was incorporated about the same time. America Online was founded in 1985 and has more than four times the net profit of Time Warner, earning $762 million in the fiscal year that ended June 30, even though Time Warner's revenues of $26.8 billion dwarf AOL's $4.8 billion." – Associated Press report[8]

- "America Online, Inc. and Time Warner Inc. today announced a strategic merger of equals to create the world's first fully integrated media and communications company for the Internet Century ... [T]his unique new enterprise will be the premier global company delivering branded information, entertainment, and communications services across rapidly converging media platforms." – AOL and Time Warner joint corporate news release[9]

- "I must say that one of the early problems this week was parsing the purposely obfuscated press release from the two companies which spun this as a merger of equals ... It took a while internally for it really to be sunk in that 55 percent of the company was owned by AOL." – CNNfn correspondent Steve Young[10]

- "According to Media Metrix, AOL's proprietary and Web-based online network attracted more than 54 million unique visitors in November [1999], far outdistancing second-place Yahoo's 41 million. When you combine AOL's totals with those of Time Warner's online properties, which exceeded 12 million visitors in November, AOL will command a market position that will be virtually impossible to topple for several years." – report in *The Wall Street Journal*[11]

- "This is the equivalent of control of the railroads in the early 20th century, but it's far more important because it's about the control of the central nervous system of our democracy." – Jeff Chester, Center on Media Education, quoted in *The Christian Science Monitor*[12]

LEAP BEFORE YOU LOOK TOO DEEPLY

A key aspect of effective leadership is knowing when to stop gathering information and make a decision. It's easy – too easy, in fact – to say that moment arrives when all the information needed for a decision is in hand. As any great military leader – Colin Powell, for example – knows, the commander who fails to act before all of the desired information is available won't be a leader for long.

Business has never been much different in requiring action with less-than-comprehensive information. But the advantages of a "bias for action" are more pronounced today than ever before. Surveying AOL's competitive position in 1995, a San Francisco analyst said, "The odds seem to be in their favor so far and their track record is second to none ... but as a rapidly growing business, there are going to be errors."[13] It's that potential for errors that scares so many managers from being decisive in the absence of full information.

Privacy experts' "worries about AOL–Time Warner's accumulating a database ... are a perverse confirmation that Case and Levin are on to something."
– Newsweek

Steve Case and his top team seem not to be among them. True, AOL's storied history of errors (reviewed in the previous chapter) is a testament to their decisions that went wrong. But AOL would not be counted today among the most valuable companies on earth if there weren't also a great many decisions that went right – and were made expeditiously enough to beat competitors to the punch.

Here, too, the merger with Time Warner serves as a recent, highly publicized object lesson. "Now these two giants are making an audacious bet that, joined together in the biggest merger ever, they will be able to resolve both their strategic pickles," *The Wall Street Journal* comments, after recounting AOL's need for content and access to high-speed cable lines and Time Warner's previously unsuccessful efforts to cope with emergence of the Internet. "The mega-deal suddenly tears down the walls between old media and new, setting the stage for a huge collision of cultures and corporate fiefdoms."[14]

Did AOL in effect panic and grab too hastily for the content- and cable-laden Time Warner while it was in a position to do so? Technology journalist Anthony B. Perkins thinks so, saying, "Case's most significant stroke of genius will be that he bought Time Warner when AOL's market value was near its overhyped peak."[15] Author Michael Lewis concurs, asserting, "Now [AOL is] stuck, just like any old company. It has gone and bought all sorts of things it could have rented much more cheaply, and safely."[16]

Anticipating the day that "the Internet gets faster and more ubiquitous," *Newsweek* holds:

> "… it's reasonable to think that the mammoth new company might indeed make a mint from its media properties … If such synergy didn't make sense, why would privacy experts already be wringing their hands about the implications of the merger? Their worries about AOL–Time Warner's accumulating a database, with everything from your reading habits to your day-trading logs, are a perverse confirmation that Case and Levin are on to something."[17]

What the arguments over the advisability of the merger demonstrate is that no one can do any more than make an educated guess at the outcome at this point, because no one – not even Steve Case and Gerald Levin and their entire top teams put together – has the information needed to be any more certain of the likely outcome. Does that make Case, Levin, *et al.* bad managers? No. Doing nothing makes bad managers.

PREPARE FOR THE DAY YOU'RE NOT NEEDED

Whatever your business is today, no matter how entrenched and unthreatened it may seem – the day will come that it dies. That's a central finding of McKinsey & Company consultants who conducted research aimed at identifying what's required to achieve consistent, profitable growth. They found "successful companies can and must outlive their individual businesses," as reported in the book *The Alchemy of Growth*. "They must grow new businesses. That's what leads to sustained, profitable growth."

Stated more succinctly: This, too, shall pass. Steve Case seems always to have at least implicitly understood the truth – and implication – of this ancient adage. When the Web appeared to threaten the viability of proprietary online services including AOL, for example, the company was prepared with a transition in services and content that made the Web an asset rather than a threat.

More recently, AOL "faces a world shifting toward high-speed Internet connections like those it could get from Time Warner's cable systems," *The Wall Street Journal* reports. Thus, the AOL–Time Warner merger "has a powerful out-with-the-old feel, and seems to represent with rare clarity one of those infrequent dividing lines between an industry's past and its future."[18]

It's a dividing line foreseen in 1999 by information-strategies consultant Jim Seymour, who wrote, "The [Internet service provider] business, *per se*, is going to become a less and less important part of computing, at least on the consumer level, over the next few years ... By then, I expect that America Online will be reincarnated as a full-fledged media company, the days of whistling modem connections, metered billing, and worries about broadband access long forgotten."[19]

It's a reincarnation that AOL itself may welcome. "Though it has styled itself a media company, it climbed to the top of the Internet industry as a glorified switchboard operator, wiring people into the online world and connecting them with Web sites," *The Wall Street Journal* says. "Amid a surge in free Internet access, more than ever AOL must rely on advertising and e-commerce, not subscription revenue, for profit."[20] Technology reporter Kara Swisher, author of the book *AOL.com*, gets more personal with the same line of thinking, asserting that Steve Case has "been very interested in the media forever ... He knew his business was not dialing up and accessing the Internet. It was about being a media company."[21]

> "[S]uccessful companies ... must grow new businesses. That's what leads to sustained, profitable growth."
> – *The Alchemy of Growth*

Whether or not Case as an individual or AOL as a company harbored any desire to join with a mainstream media empire, the rise and fall that inevitably is part of the history of any commercial endeavor drove them to consider corporate life in light of coming dramatic changes in interactivity. The merger they fashioned in response would seem to gain favor of the

McKinsey consultants, who write that in a proposed merger, "The question would be whether the two companies together grow more quickly than they would have separately. That would be the case if the two companies find ways to benefit from the capabilities that each brings to the deal ... Put the capabilities together and maybe you have a mega-company that will grow faster than the two would have by themselves."[22]

Of course, merger is but one way to deal with the inevitable death of businesses. The critical requirement is to deal with it.

NEVER CEASE "PURSUIT OF THE IDEA"

Steve Case has been self-motivated in the extreme his entire life. His brother Dan recalls Steve waking him up in the middle of the night with the perfect name for yet another entrepreneurial undertaking the siblings were planning. Asked by *Business Week* why a kid in very comfortable circumstances would be brimming with ideas for making money, Steve replies, "It was the challenge, the pursuit of the idea."[23]

> "... no one here is congratulating themselves. We're totally focused on the future."
> – Steve Case

That pursuit rocketed Case to the peak of global enterprise less than 30 years after he peddled papers, magazines, and watches as a kid and – in the transition to chairmanship of AOL Time Warner – a new approach to pursuit of the idea: "The role I'm going to play is, I think, the role I can play best," he said at the merger announcement press conference. "Certainly the one I enjoy the most is really being a strategist, thinking about maybe what might be looming around the corners without having to be burdened by what's happening today or this week or this month or this quarter."[24]

He could appropriately have added a comment he made five years earlier, a thought that might serve any executive as well as it's served Steve Case: "Despite all our growth and the rise in our stock price, no one here is congratulating themselves. We're totally focused on the future."[25]

GET TO THE FUTURE TODAY

Your customers no longer care – or need – to wait for supply to catch up with their demands; they want what they want when they want it, which is now. That's what AOL has been doing for years – though many outside observers seem not to have caught on to the company's gambit. Here are the steps that can make your company a similarly speedy responder to today's more demanding consumer:

- *Be willing to be wrong – for now.* If you anticipate customers' future wants exactly right – as AOL has done so often – you'll at first have a new product with no takers, but lots of critics guffawing over your bonehead strategy. At first, but not for long.

- *Leap before you look too deeply.* Waiting to know all you could know before committing to a course of action can be the commercial kiss of death in a world moving as fast as yours is today. AOL has succeeded more often than not with its decisions by making them expeditiously and accepting the inevitability of occasionally misfiring.

- *Prepare for the day you're not needed.* The only thing that lasts in business today is change. Whatever you have to sell today, no matter how successful, will someday be unwanted in an ever-changing marketplace. Your choice must be – like AOL's – to constantly explore, nurture, and develop new lines of business.

- *Never cease "pursuit of the idea."* The way to success, wealth, and power, Steve Case-style, is not to pursue success, wealth, and power, but inner motivation. It's a course we all should follow.

NOTES

1. Michael Lewis, "AOL: Almost Obscenely Large," *The Wall Street Journal*, January 13, 2000.

2. Alexandra Marks and Ron Scherer, "Merger a Landmark of Cyber Age," *The Christian Science Monitor*, January 11, 2000.

3. Fred Vogelstein, "The Talented Mr. Case," *US News & World Report*, January 24, 2000.

4. Joshua Cooper Ramo, "How AOL Lost the Battles but Won the War," *Time*, September 22,1997.

5. Amy Cortese and Amy Barrett, "The Online World of Steve Case," *Business Week*, April 15,1996.

6. Holman W. Jenkins Jr, "The Last Crazy Internet Valuation?" *The Wall Street Journal*, January 12, 2000.

7. Martin Peers, Nick Wingfield, and Laura Landro, "AOL and Time Warner Leap Boundaries to Join in Mammoth Merger," *The Wall Street Journal*, January 11, 2000.

8. Seth Sutel, "AOL to Buy Time Warner for $166B," AP Online, January 10, 2000.

9. AOL–Time Warner joint corporate news release, January 10, 2000.

10. CNN television network, "Reliable Sources," January 15, 2000.

11. Anthony B. Perkins, "AOL Beats the Odds – Again," *The Wall Street Journal*, January 12, 2000.

12. Alexandra Marks and Ron Scherer, "Merger a Landmark of Cyber Age," *The Christian Science Monitor*, January 11, 2000.

13. Kara Swisher, "Steve Case Tries to Hold a Place Online," *The Washington Post*, August 27, 1995.

14. Thomas E. Weber, Martin Peers, and Nick Wingfield, "Two Titans in a Strategic Bind Bet on a Futuristic Mega-deal," *The Wall Street Journal*, January 11, 2000.

15. Anthony B. Perkins, "AOL Beats the Odds – Again," *The Wall Street Journal*, January 12, 2000.

16. Michael Lewis, "AOL: Almost Obscenely Large," *The Wall Street Journal*, January 13, 2000.

17. Steven Levy, "The Two Big Bets," *Newsweek*, January 24, 2000.

18. Martin Peers, Nick Wingfield, and Laura Landro, "AOL and Time Warner Leap Boundaries to Join in Mammoth Merger," *The Wall Street Journal*, January 11, 2000.

19. Jim Seymour, "Why AOL Will Be Just Fine, Thanks," *TheStreet.com*, May 25, 1999.

20. Thomas E. Weber, Martin Peers, and Nick Wingfield, "Two Titans in a Strategic Bind Bet on a Futuristic Mega-deal," *The Wall Street Journal*, January 11, 2000.

21. CNN television network, "Reliable Sources," January 15, 2000.

22. Stephen Coley, Mehrdad Baghai, and David White, *The Alchemy of Growth*, Perseus, Cambridge, Massachusetts, 1999.

23. Amy Cortese and Amy Barrett, "The Online World of Steve Case," *Business Week*, April 15,1996.

24. Rajiv Chandrasekaran, "A Case of Timing, Knowledge," *The Washington Post*, January 11, 2000.

25. Steve Lohr, "Steve Case at a Crossroad," *The New York Times*, August 14, 1995.

HOW TO SUCCEED THE AOL WAY

At the beginning of the 1990s, America Online existed only as a struggling online service, owned by an obscure company called Quantum Computer Services, that provided limited games, e-mail, chat rooms, and news articles to computer owners. By the end of that decade – after a corporate name change and 1992 initial public offering – AOL's stock market value placed it among the world's largest companies. The CNN network's "Moneyline" program named AOL "Stock of the Decade," with a best-in-the-US appreciation of almost 69,000 percent.

How has AOL achieved such remarkable results? A thorough examination of reports and commentary on the company since its inception points to the 10 keys to success described in preceding pages. Here they are again, with brief explanations intended to guide you in taking your firm or unit to AOL-like heights:

1. Go into everybody's business

You can no longer soar to success in buggy whips and similar anachronistic lines of work, so it's smart to offer customers something you can reasonably expect they'll need. If you do, the principal early challenges are to overcome early discouragement, learn from initial failures and triumphs alike, and be willing to make course corrections in everything but your dream.

2. Give your business a human face

Steve Case, unlike most other leaders of the technological revolution, understood from the outset that his business, like all others, is ultimately a people business. He proves the tremendous value of recognizing that all of a company's stakeholders – employees, customers, shareholders, and oneself – are individuals, and their overriding aim is to feel connected with others.

3. Never be dissuaded from pursuing your dream

Steve Case's excellent adventure with AOL has been no cakewalk; rather, he's been doubted and second-guessed every step of the way. His experience and AOL's history demonstrate that you can come out a winner by staying firmly fixed on achieving your vision.

4. KISS!

Too many businesses get so caught up it their own prowess and sophistication that they fail to KISS: keep it simple, stupid! A large measure of AOL's success can be simply attributed to simplicity, which the company maintained while so many others made things too tough on customers. The difficult challenge of making things ever-easier on users is the smart way to go for every enterprise.

5. Ignore "irrelevant" experts – customers rule!

We're experts in what we do for a living – who else knows as much about our products and services? The urge, therefore, is to give customers what we think they *should* want. It's a mistake companies make again and again, but AOL has avoided like the plague. The company's success from doing so is a dramatic illustration that customers know best what customers want.

6. Don't shy from a fight ...

Steve Case's leadership shows that nice guys don't finish last, but first, provided they fight their business battles under today's changed rules of corporate competition. That means selectively choosing where and how to take a stand, staying focused on business aims rather than competitive foes, and employing the natural advantages of the company's size – whether it's small or large.

7 ...Or hesitate to sleep with the enemy

In this Internet age, no company can keep up on its own with the knowledge explosion, changing markets, or shifting customer demands. AOL shows the way things have got to be done: you purchase and partner as required – even in league with your presumed chief competitor – to grow your company, advance its mission, and succeed in these challenging times.

8. Leverage successes, build your brands

AOL's relatively short corporate existence vividly demonstrates that even a high-achieving company can't let down its guard or take a breather to enjoy its accomplishments – old and new competitors are always gunning for you. You've got to extend and solidify your brands, leverage past success with new initiatives, and win an increasing customer share and share of customers.

9. Admit mistakes and grow forward

AOL hasn't grown despite mistakes, it's made mistakes that are part and parcel of any ambitious growth effort. There's a graveyard-worth of deceased companies that never made attention-grabbing blunders. Your firm is unlikely to join them if you accept reasonable risks, take occasional lumps, and soar on the strength of your wins.

10. Get to the future today

Winning companies today are the ones, like AOL, that are ready with what customers want before the customers know they want it. If you're among them, you'll shrug off the invective hurled at market leaders, repeatedly display your bias for action, anticipate where changes in customer preferences are heading, and always keep focused on your dream.

A HEADLONG RUSH INTO THE UNKNOWN

I f you believe the pundits and prognosticators, AOL is heading for corporate power and riches of unimaginable proportions in the years ahead. Or the company is heading for the graveyard of enterprises that haughtily supposed past success could be extended and compounded indefinitely, only to find themselves six feet under and unlamented.

Take your pick. And while you're at it, take your pick concerning your own company as well. Because uncertainty on a vast scale reigns supreme in business today. Any manager is in a headlong rush into the unknown.

Management consultant Christopher Meyer, co-author of *Blur: The Speed of Change in the Connected Economy*, envisions your situation this way: "You're perched on a bridge, staring into the abyss. Your center of gravity seems to be in two places: your head, and thoughts, directed toward the uncertain bungee jump you're about to make; your feet planted on the ledge of the bridge, tethered to it only by the bungee cord." Meyer says,

"That's where the world is today, anchored in the present but looking toward its uncertain future."[1]

And uncertainty is unnerving. But – as demonstrated by human fascination with horror movies, roller coasters, and extreme sports like bungee jumping – it can also be thrilling. In business, the thrill depends on such matters as your attitude toward competition, tolerance of risk, and confidence in your vision of how things should be.

These matters and more can be favorably affected by learning well from AOL's secrets of success. The company overcame uncertainty on a scale that few firms have so decidedly overcome – only to face the further uncertainty that confronts every business today, as it stares into the abyss that is the future.

Take a cue from Steve Case, who – although weary from the packed week in which the AOL–Time Warner merger was announced – could still anticipate the uncertain future by insisting that his company's story was just starting. "Okay, maybe it's chapter four now," he admits. "But only chapter four."[2]

NOTES

1.   Author interview.

2.   Kara Swisher, "How Steve Case Morphed Into a Media Mogul," *The Wall Street Journal*, January 11, 2000.

INDEX